LONDON & SOUTH WESTERN RAILWAY
MISCELLANY

Old Waterloo c1900, with Adams 'X2' 4-4-0 No 680 about to depart with an express for the South and an 'M7' 0-4-4T awaiting its next turn of duty in an adjacent platform, this particular 'M7' has an experimental conical smokebox door, as fitted to several examples of the class when new. On the left of the picture another Adams tender locomotive takes water. *Lens of Sutton collection*

In memory of my father, Glyn Morgan
(4 August 1906 - 13 September 2002).
We travelled far together,
and both experienced the wonder
of our railway heritage.

LONDON & SOUTH WESTERN RAILWAY
MISCELLANY
John Scott-Morgan

OPC

An imprint of
Ian Allan Publishing

CLAPHAM CUTTING

No 419

Contents

Acknowledgements

I should like to thank the following for their kind help in the compilation of this book: Roger Carpenter, Richard Stumpf, Rod Blencoe, Tom Middlemass, Deric Sprange, John Boas, David Rose and Alan Blackburn, for their help with photographs; also the Locomotive Club of Great Britain, the Ken Nunn collection, Guildford Museum, and Peter Waller, Alan Butcher, Paul Cripps, Lawrie Bowles and Nick Grant of Ian Allan Publishing, for their kind patience during the production of this book. Finally, my thanks must go to Claire Turnbull for typing the manuscript.

Bibliography

LSWR Locomotives, Volumes 1 and 2, D. L. Bradley
    (RCTS, 1965 and 1967);
The LSWR, Volumes 1 and 2, R. A. Williams
    (David & Charles, 1968 and 1973);
The LSWR in the 20th Century, R. A. Williams and
    John Faulkner (David & Charles, 1988);
The South Western Railway, C. Hamilton-Ellis
    (George Allen & Unwin, 1956);
Railway and other Steamers, C. L. D. Duckworth and
    G. E. Langmuir (Stephenson Publishing, 1948);
The LSWR, G. A. Sekon
    (published privately, 1896);
Sir Herbert Walker's Southern Railway, C. F. Klapper
    (Ian Allan Publishing, 1973);
Twenty Locomotive Men, C. Hamilton-Ellis
    (George Allen & Unwin, 1957);
LSWR Locomotives, H. C. Casserley
    (Ian Allan Publishing, 1971);
Pre-Grouping Atlas and Gazetteer, compiled by P. Connolly
    (Ian Allan Publishing, 1976);
Steam from Waterloo, Col H. C. B. Rogers
    (David & Charles, 1985).

Title page:
A down West of England restaurant-car express headed by Drummond 'L12' 4-4-0 No 419 passing Clapham Cutting intermediate 'box *c*1910. This example of the 'L12' class was built at Nine Elms in 1904 and had 6ft 7in driving wheels. The train is made up of LSWR panelled bogie stock designed by Surrey Warner. *Ian Allan Library*

Introduction

Pullman at sunset

On a summer's day, long ago in 1956 (or was it 1957?) my father and I stood at the end of the platform at Waterloo which led from the carriage road. As we waited, a small 'G6' 0-6-0T appeared with a train of Pullman cars marked up for the 'Bournemouth Belle'. After they had arrived in the adjacent platform, the voluminous form of a Bulleid 'Merchant Navy' Pacific backed down on to the train. After watering, its path was set and the train was given the road. With a thundering roar, the 'Boxpoc' wheels of this mighty giant spun and clouds of grey smoke churned skywards from its large chimney. Presently the locomotive found its feet and the Pullman train eased out of the station, passing over the crossovers, around the long curve at the approach of the station and then out of sight on its way to Vauxhall and southwards on the first leg of its journey to Bournemouth. This, then, was my first experience of the railway that was once the London & South Western.

The London & South Western Railway

Unlike the British people of today, who are in the main timid in their approach to great projects, the late Georgians and early Victorians had great courage and a huge capacity to learn new ideas through calculated risk-taking, which led to Britain's becoming a leader in all things connected with engineering and science. With all the petty-minded bureaucrats that we encounter in this day and age, it is very hard to imagine a group of enlightened people projecting a railway like the London & Southampton, with all the geographical and civil-engineering problems encountered in the 1830s.

The first public meeting of the London & Southampton Railway was held at Southampton in April 1831, chaired by Colonel Henderson; during the meeting it was noted that the railway company would purchase five locomotives at a cost of £500 each — two for passenger and three for goods traffic. Henderson stated that the land to build the line would cost £65,000, at £100 an acre, and that an estimated 84 acres would be needed for each station on the line. It was further remarked that the permanent-way materials would last at least 30 years.

The success of the Stockton & Darlington and the Liverpool & Manchester railways spurred on the potential backers of the London & Southampton. The project was a brave one, in that Southampton was then but a small fishing port at the mouth of the rivers Test and Itchen, with a population of 19,000 inhabitants, and that the only town or city of any size along the whole stretch of line from London to Southampton was Winchester, with a population of 8,000. The hopes and dreams of the investors were sorely tested on many occasions at this time.

The original scheme to build the line was entitled 'The Southampton, London & Branch Railway & Docks' — a clumsy name, to say the least — with a capital of £1,500,000. This early scheme was thrown out by Parliament, as were further modified proposals, until the passing of the London & Birmingham Railway Act in 1833, after which the backers of the Southampton project gained new strength and enthusiasm for the project. A fresh approach was made, resulting in the passing of an Act to build the line, on 25 July 1834.

With a capital of £1 million and loans of £330,000, the construction of the London & Southampton Railway was begun. The cost was £894,874, with 11.5% being added to the stock for contingencies for the 76¾-mile long line. From its Nine Elms terminus the line took a southwesterly route via Wimbledon, Surbiton (Kingston), Woking Common, Farnborough and Fleet as far as Basingstoke, where it tuned due south to Winchester and Southampton. The railway's first engineer was Francis Giles, who was also engineer of the Basingstoke Canal; its first architect was William Tite, who designed all the major buildings along the route. During

At an unknown location deep in the country (believed to be near Andover), an 'H13' railcar approaches a lattice signal as it coasts down the gradient with a local service. *Ian Allan Library*

Giles's time a line would also be surveyed from Basingstoke to Exeter via Salisbury and Honiton, with branches to Newbury and Oxford; the Basingstoke-Exeter stretch would later be built in stages and opened progressively from July 1854 to July 1860.

In 1836 the company asked George and Robert Stephenson to survey routes to Bristol from Basingstoke and to Taunton from Salisbury. This brought the Southampton company into conflict with the newly formed Great Western Railway, which at that time had not laid a yard of track. The bad feeling would remain between the two companies for all time.

Construction of the London & Southampton main line proved difficult, as Francis Giles had engaged small firms of contractors to build certain sections. This practice was all well and good when the formation was easy, but when the going became difficult these small firms, with almost no proper capital, often had a hard time and nearly always asked for the contract to be re-evaluated, to take into account the civil-engineering problems.

As a result of the problems and also of bad management, in January 1837 the directors replaced Giles with Joseph Locke, who came to the project with considerable skill and knowledge, being a pupil of George Stephenson. One of his first actions was to replace the small contractors working on the line from Nine Elms to Woking with the firm run by Thomas Brassey, then a newcomer to the railway contracting fraternity. Locke was to complete the project and overcome the difficulties posed by the civil-engineering problems, especially those between Basingstoke and Winchester. At Fleet Pond, north of Basingstoke, the line had been built across the stretch of water using a carpet of willow branches and then banked with sand and gravel inlay. A second section of the line that caused trouble was from Basingstoke, south to Winchester. This part of the alignment entailed tunnels north of Andover Road (Micheldever). This work took a considerable length of time, due to the conditions of the ground and also the chalk which kept on caving in.

One person of note who became involved with the railway at this time was William James Chaplin, the principal partner in Chaplin & Horne, which had extensive coaching and hotel interests. Chaplin was a man who had an eye for the future and subscribed to the company at a very early stage. He quickly decided to sell all his main interests in the coaching company and became a director of the London & Southampton Railway.

The first official train ran from Nine Elms to Woking Common on 12 May 1838. After the crossing of Fleet Pond, the next section to be opened was between Woking Common and Winchfield, on 29 September 1838, followed by a further extension, to Basingstoke, on 12 June 1839.

The section of line from Southampton to Winchester was also opened on 12 June 1839, leaving a gap between Basingstoke and Winchester, which was served by a road coach service, the journey taking two hours between the two locations. The connection between Basingstoke and Winchester was completed in May 1840, the line being opened as a through route on 11 May 1840.

There had always been a rivalry between Southampton and Portsmouth, the good people of Portsmouth indicating that they would rather have no railway at all than a line with 'Southampton' in its title. As a result of this feeling by the company's potential passengers and freight customers, the London & Southampton Railway changed its name, by an Act of Parliament passed on 4 June 1839, to the London & South Western Railway (LSWR), with a share capital of £300,000.

The next important development, in May 1840, was the proposal of a route from Bishopstoke (Eastleigh) to Gosport. The line, via Fareham, was duly opened on 29 November 1841 but had to be temporarily closed two days later as a result of geological problems with a tunnel near Fareham and did not reopen to passenger traffic until 7 February 1842. This almost broke Thomas Brassey and left Locke fearing for his reputation. Neither the people of Portsmouth nor the military had much to be proud of, as both had prevented the railway from being built to a location in Portsmouth itself, the local people having favoured a line to London via Arundel and Horsham connected to the Brighton company, and the military taking a paranoid view that such a railway project would damage the fortification of Portsmouth and allow possible invasion of the town.

As we have already seen, the LSWR had firm plans to expand in the west and also looked on more than one occasion towards the east and north. In 1844 the company put before Parliament bills to construct lines to Guildford from Woking, to Newbury from Basingstoke and to Weymouth from Southampton via Dorchester.

The branch to Guildford was originally promoted by a small private company called the Guildford Junction Railway and was to be laid using wooden rails, according to the Prosser Patent System of Guided Trains. The Board was very concerned about this proposal and insisted that one of the lines on the double track to Guildford be laid in iron rails, so as not to interfere with through traffic. In the event, the line was laid throughout with iron rails and the company was acquired by the LSWR soon after it opened on 5 May 1845, thus presenting opportunities for expansion south to Portsmouth and the South Coast. A further extension, from Guildford to Godalming, was opened in October 1849.

There followed a protracted and complicated series of negotiations which came about as a result of the Portsmouth Direct Railway being promoted as an independent line in 1853 by Thomas Brassey, the contractor offering the line to any railway company willing to operate it. At first the LSWR was very reluctant to operate the line, owing to its arrangements with the LBSCR, which already ran trains to Portsmouth, so Brassey approached the South Eastern Railway, which operated a line from Tonbridge to Reading via Guildford. Negotiations between the SER and Brassey were at an advanced stage when the LSWR decided to purchase the line as a blocking move to stop a third railway reaching Portsmouth. This situation led to bad feeling between the LSWR and the Brighton company, in turn leading to the so-called Battle of Havant, which occurred at the junction, just east of Havant station, where the Portsmouth Direct line met the LBSCR coastal line to Brighton; both companies chained locomotives to the track, and gangs of navvies removed sections of rail and also part of the junction. It was originally advertised that the first train would run on 1 January 1859. However, because of this unfortunate situation, the whole business became a matter for the Courts, and, as a result, the first train did not run until 24 January. Nevertheless, the LSWR now had a direct route to Portsmouth from London, with joint running powers over the line from Havant to Portsmouth.

In July 1860 the LSWR reached Exeter through a series of extensions — firstly via a branch from Bishopstoke to Salisbury, which opened on 1 March 1847, and later by a direct line from Basingstoke to Salisbury via Andover, opened on 1 May 1857. Extensions from Salisbury to Exeter were built in stages, firstly to Yeovil, following which a further Act gave the LSWR the right to build a double-track main line from Dorchester to Exeter or a single-track main line from Yeovil to Exeter via Honiton; the directors decided on the Yeovil-Exeter route, which was double-tracked at a later date.

For the LSWR one of the most important towns on the South Coast was Bournemouth. The first route to Bournemouth ran from Northam to Brockenhurst, onward to Ringwood and from there to Poole and Hamworthy, entailing a very long and protracted journey for any passenger wishing to travel to the resort. This situation was much improved by the construction of the direct line from Brockenhurst to Bournemouth via Christchurch, which opened on 14 March 1870; this followed the completion of a branch from Ringwood to Christchurch via Hurn, opened on 13 November 1862.

The LSWR had always had designs on the far South West of England, with an interest in constructing lines to Devon and Cornwall. The company's main rival, the Great Western, deeply resented this and was determined to keep the LSWR out of its territory. The GWR's interests in the South West were made up of the South Devon and the Cornwall Railway, both built to Brunel's broad gauge.

In August 1845, by way of a project to build a series of lines in North Devon and Cornwall as the Cornwall & Devon Central Railway, the LSWR had purchased the Bodmin & Wadebridge Railway, one of Britain's earliest railways. At this time, this was a good 200 miles from the nearest LSWR railhead, and it was not until 1 July 1886 that Parliamentary sanction was obtained by the LSWR to incorporate the line. Thus it was that for over 40 years the LSWR had to transport by sea all materials and any new rolling stock to/from this isolated line.

The distrust and hostility between the Great Western and the London & South Western was further inflamed in February 1847, when the latter purchased a large number of shares in the fledgling Exeter & Crediton Railway. This six-mile-long broad-gauge branch, considered part of the Bristol & Exeter empire, was acquired by the LSWR, which regarded it as a very useful route for its proposed lines to North Devon and Cornwall. Over the next 50 years the company would build a network of main and branch lines from Exeter into the heart of Devon and on to North Devon and Cornwall.

A further line acquired by the LSWR as a broad-gauge project was the Taw Vale & Crediton Railway, which was projected to run from Crediton to Barnstaple. As the directors would have nothing to do with the Bristol & Exeter Railway and favoured the LSWR instead, the company found life quite hard when, as a result of its being projected as a broad-gauge line, the Gauge Commissioners refused to allow its construction as a standard-gauge railway. The Taw Vale directors then approached the Bristol & Exeter Railway for help but were refused.

The LSWR's development from Exeter into North Devon and Cornwall was long and protracted, the situation exacerbated by the Great Western and its constituent companies, which were intent on keeping as much as possible of the West Country for themselves. The Taw Vale changed its name to the North Devon Railway, opening on 1 August 1854; ironically, Thomas Brassey, who had originally leased this and the Exeter & Crediton Railway, eventually subcontracted the Bristol & Exeter to work both lines on his behalf. Both the North Devon Railway and the Bideford Extension Railway — an independent broad-gauge line opened on 2 November 1855 — would be amalgamated with the LSWR on 1 January 1865, the Exeter & Crediton following in 1879.

Extension of the line from Nine Elms to Waterloo commenced in July 1846. This 2¼-mile stretch, consisting of four tracks and involving the construction of 300 brick arches between Nine Elms and Waterloo Road, would eventually cost the company £2 million. The first train to run into the new station arrived from Southampton at 4.30am on 13 July 1848, and from that day the original terminus at Nine Elms closed to passenger traffic, remaining open only for freight. The company also had the foresight to purchase a further 12 acres at Waterloo, for any future extensions, which would come in useful when the station was rebuilt early in the 20th century.

In 1847 the company started work on promoting a line to Windsor from Richmond and also constructing a loop line to Hounslow via Barnes, Chiswick and Brentford. A great race then commenced between the Great Western and the LSWR to reach Windsor first, which the Great Western won! The line from Richmond to Windsor was opened to Datchet on 22 August 1848 and the Brentford to Barnes loop opened in August 1849. A further extension from Datchet to Windsor Newtown was opened to a permanent station on 1 May 1851.

The LSWR entered into an agreement with the North London Railway to allow through running from the North London's line from South Acton to Richmond via Kew Bridge and Barnes, where trains had to be reversed; this commenced on 20 May 1858, loop lines later being built at Kew and Barnes to improve this service. From 1 January 1869 NLR trains used the new route from South Acton Junction to Richmond, via Gunnersbury, over part of the LSWR Richmond branch via Kensington Addison Road. The joint agreement with the North London was largely a reaction to a proposal by the Great Western to build a branch from Brentford to Richmond, which project duly failed.

Following its failure to build a line to Bristol in the 1840s, the LSWR's main interests seemed to be the construction of lines to Devon and Cornwall. However, the opportunity was not missed to acquire, with the Midland Railway, the joint ownership of the Somerset & Dorset Railway, which became a joint undertaking from 1 November 1875. This gave both the Midland and the LSWR routes from Bath to the South Coast, which gave both companies greater traffic potential. The company also had a close relationship in the Midland & South Western Junction Railway, which ran from Andover, in Hampshire, to Andoversford, near Cheltenham. Like the Somerset & Dorset, this line had been built in stages (under different titles), from the 1860s until the 1880s but, despite its close relationship with the LSWR, would become part of the Great Western Railway at the Grouping.

The development of the LSWR system and its expansion into the major railway that it was eventually to become started in the late 1870s and continued until the outbreak of World War 1 in 1914. During this period the company extended not only its railway interest, but also its shipping and port ownership, the LSWR taking over the Southampton Harbour Co in 1892. The company duly built up a fine fleet of ships and ran services to the Isle of Wight, in conjunction with the LBSCR, and also to the Channel Islands and French

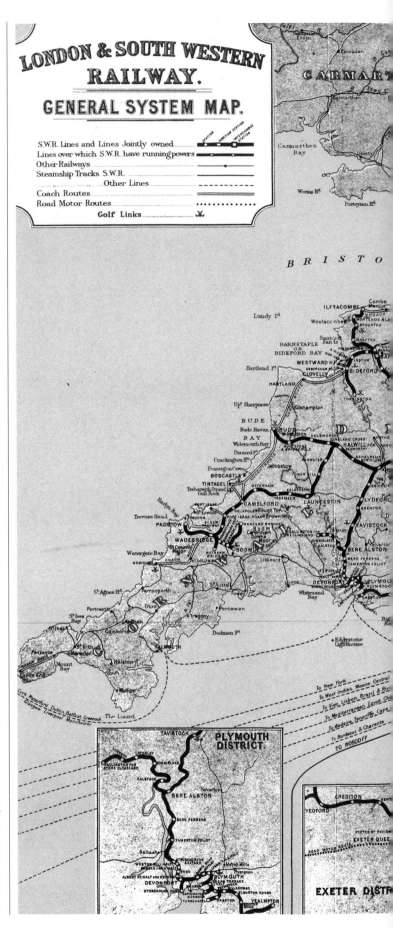

8

Drummond 'T14' 4-6-0 No 447 approaches Weybridge with an up express on 7 August 1911. These locomotives were the best of a bad lot and were later rebuilt by Robert Urie with superheated boilers. The last members of the class were not withdrawn from service until 1951. *R. C. Stumpf collection*

ports. In 1923 the Southern Railway would inherit from the LSWR a fleet of passenger and cargo ships and combine this with those of the LBSCR and SECR to form its Marine Department.

Towards the end of the 19th century the LSWR penetrated further into Devon and Cornwall, building lines to Bude, which opened on 10 August 1898, and finally to Padstow via Wadebridge, opened on 27 March 1899. Both reached the Atlantic coast via Okehampton, which was also an important junction point for the line south to Tavistock and Plymouth, with its sizeable dock complex.

The final contributions in terms of track mileage centred around the construction of two blocking lines, primarily to keep the Great Western out of Hampshire. The Basingstoke & Alton Light Railway was opened in 1900 to prevent the GWR going south from Basingstoke towards Portsmouth; the Meon Valley line from Alton to Fareham, as well as frustrating the GWR's plans for eastward expansion, was intended as a route for military traffic and opened on 1 June 1903 (coincidentally the same day as that from Budleigh Salterton to Exmouth). Neither would yield any real revenue for the LSWR, the Basingstoke & Alton Light Railway closing to all traffic on 1 January 1917. Following much debate it would be restored after World War 1, only to be closed again in 1936.

At the beginning of the 20th century the LSWR was very much involved in minor railways. One of these was the Axminster-Lyme Regis branch, construction of which commenced in 1900 and was completed ready for opening on 24 August 1903. Another example of co-operation with a minor company involved the Plymouth, Devonport & South Western Junction Railway, which, by an agreement of 24 October 1883, ran a line from Lydford to Devonport

and gave the LSWR access to Plymouth. The PDSWJR later constructed a branch from Bere Alston to Callington Road along the route of the erstwhile 4ft-gauge East Cornwall Mineral Railway, and this opened on 2 March 1908. The PDSWJR was finally taken over by the LSWR only in 1922, in preparation for the Grouping. On the Isle of Wight, the LSWR had joint interests (with the LBSCR) in the Ryde Pier Co and the Isle of Wight Steam Packet Co; these included the line from Ryde Pier Head to Ryde St Johns Road station, worked by the Isle of Wight Railway.

The LSWR had a good relationship with the military, which it served with several connecting lines to military railways. Perhaps the most important of these was the Woolmer Instructional Military Railway at Longmoor Camp in Hampshire, which was used for instructing sappers of the Royal Engineers in railway operation. The company also had connections with the Amesbury Camp Light Railway on Salisbury Plain, opened in 1901, and the Fovant Camp line, and all three were to hire or purchase ex-LSWR locomotives or stock at some time or other.

As the LSWR progressed from the late 19th century to the early 20th century, great changes were afoot, in terms not only of locomotive and rolling stock but also of the way the company was administered at Waterloo; probably the two finest General Managers the company ever had were Sir Sam Fay and Herbert Ascombe Walker, both of whom contributed greatly to the advancement of the company during this period.

In the last decade of its existence the LSWR started a project to electrify the London suburban system. Already, on 1 January 1907, the company had taken over the Waterloo & City Railway, in which it had had a major financial interest from its opening on 11 July 1898.

The first surface-line electrification had been effected in conjunction with the District Railway under an Act of 1901 to electrify the line from Putney to Wimbledon. This line opened to electric services on 27 August 1905 and used the most northerly platforms at Wimbledon. The next stage of development entailed the District Railway's electrifying the LSWR suburban line from Studland Road, Hammersmith, to Richmond via Turnham Green. The District Railway began its electrified Ealing service on 1 July 1905, followed by electrified services to Richmond on 1 August 1905. The electrification of the Richmond line contributed to the demise of the LSWR suburban services to Richmond via Addison Road, Kensington, which since the mid-1860s had enjoyed a wide range of services, from Waterloo, Ludgate Hill and Clapham Junction. By 5 June 1916, when the final services ran, frequency had decreased from a train every 10 minutes to a railmotor every hour. The company's services from Kingston to Tulse Hill via Wimbledon were similarly withdrawn on 1 January 1917, as a wartime economy.

Competition from electric tramways and the electrified District Railway were making serious inroads into the LSWR's profits, and, to try and stem the decline, the company decided to commence a programme of electrification. Herbert Walker thus authorised Herbert Jones, the company's Chief Electrical Engineer, to go to New York and study how the Americans had electrified their suburban railways. Jones' report was submitted to the Board on 6 December 1912, together with comments from Herbert Walker. The result was an agreement to electrify the LSWR's suburban network in two stages. Stage 1 involved Kingston Roundabout and East Putney, the Hounslow Loop, Malden–Hampton Court and Strawberry Hill–Teddington–Shepperton; Stage 2 would add Hampton Court Junction–Woking–Guildford, Hampton Court Junction–Cobham–Guildford and Raynes Park-Epsom–Effingham Junction. Traction supply would be 600V DC, by means of third-rail pick-up. A power station was to be built at Durnsford Road, Wimbledon, where there would also be a car depot; a second car depot would be built later at Effingham Junction, opened for the extension to Guildford over the new line.

Due to wartime shortages and supply problems, it was not until 25 October 1915 that electric services began, between Waterloo and Wimbledon via East Putney, followed by those to Kingston Roundabout via Raynes Park on 30 January 1916. Services commenced on the Hounslow Loop on 12 March 1916 and to Hampton Court on 18 June 1916, but those to Claygate had to wait until 20 November 1916.

Claygate to Guildford and the other Stage 2 lines were electrified in 1925.

As a result of electrification, the Locomotive Committee decided in January 1916 that the locomotive fleet could be reduced from 946 to 890. The final cost of electrification totalled £1,365,055, of which £1,186,963 was charged to capital.

The last years of the company were to bring changes that would have astounded the men who met in the 1830s and planned the London & Southampton. During the 1880s William Adams had designed some of the most handsome locomotives to grace the rails of any railway, and in the 1890s Dugald Drummond had continued this tradition, with some impressive examples of locomotive engineering. However, it was probably Robert Urie who above all designed the machines that took the LSWR into the early 20th century, and his work, together with Drummond's smaller designs, maintained an LSWR presence until the mid-1960s. In the early and middle years of the 19th century William Beattie had designed not only locomotives but also carriages and wagons, to be followed by William Panter and Surrey Warner, both of whom designed some of the finest bogie carriage stock on any British railway, some of which survived until the late 1950s and early 1960s. Similarly, the three-car electric units designed by Arthur Jones lasted until the late 1950s, albeit re-formed as four-car units.

Perhaps the LSWR's greatest single achievement was the complete rebuilding of Waterloo station, which took place in stages between 1900 and 1922. Such a monumental task, so bravely undertaken. Its design was largely in the hands of A. W. Szlumper, Chief Engineer from 1914, who had to contend not only with the complicated work of reconstruction but also with undertaking such a task in the middle of World War 1. The work was not completed until 1922, when this great station and lasting monument to the LSWR was opened on 21 March by Queen Mary.

It is now 80 years since the LSWR passed into history, and much has changed — not all for the better. No longer can one board a train at Waterloo and travel to the far reaches of Devon and North Cornwall beyond Exeter on the LSWR route. No longer are the docks at Southampton owned by the railway. There has been so much political interference with things that politicians so seldom understand and so much skulduggery by people on the make for themselves that I sometimes wonder if, in the land that gave railways to the world, there is a future for this great form of transport. Perhaps we should take heart from the example of William James Chaplin, who in 1834 had the courage to sell his coaching interests and put his faith in the railway that was to become the London & South Western.

John Scott-Morgan
Woking
March 2003

Early history, 1838-1880

Left:
Queen Victoria alights from her four-wheel Royal Saloon of 1844 at Gosport station. The occasion was the state visit to England of King Louis Philippe of France in October of that year, this being his return journey and the Royal Saloons' first. Both the four-wheel Royal Saloons were sold later to the PDSWJR and, later still, to Colonel Stephens. *Ian Allan Library*

Right:
No 13 *Orion*, a 2-2-2WT built by Sharp Brothers in 1852, at Chard Junction with a train of Beattie four-wheeled carriage stock *c*1860s. At this time the LSWR, like so many developing railways, had a hotch-potch of locomotives and rolling stock. Note the station built of local stone and the locals dressed in their Sunday best for a photograph. *Ian Allan Library*

Left:
'Hercules' class 2-4-0 No 31 *Leeds*, as modified in 1865. These passenger locomotives with 5ft 6in-diameter driving wheels were ordered by C. V. Gooch before his departure to the Eastern Counties Railway. They lasted in service until 1884, and the boiler from No 40 *Windsor* was used at Nine Elms wheelwright's shop until 1893. *Ian Allan Library*

Built at Nine Elms in 1859, 2-2-2 No 153 *Victoria* was the last express-passenger Single built for the LSWR and had 6ft 6in wheels, the cab being added later. The locomotive was the last of the 'Canute' class to be withdrawn, on 17 September 1884, and was broken up the following June. *Ian Allan Library*

The very last 'Canute' to be broken up was No 150 *Havelock*, withdrawn in June 1876 and used as a stationary boiler at Nine Elms until November 1881. *Ian Allan Library*

Below:
Beattie 2-4-0WT No 190 at Kensington Addison Road in 1872 with a train of Beattie four-wheel stock forming a train to Richmond via Hammersmith. This once-important suburban route suffered intense competition from electric trains at the start of the 20th century, and the service ceased on 5 June 1916, as a wartime economy measure. *Ian Allan Library*

Similar to the Nine Elms-built 'Lion' class, outside-framed Beyer Peacock goods 0-6-0 No 274 stands at Milford Yard, Exeter, in the 1870s. *Ian Allan Library*

THE FREEMASONS' SCHOOL, BATTERSEA RISE.

Above:
A stylised drawing of a train passing the Freemasons' School, Battersea Rise, on its way to Southampton, with a 2-2-2 inside-cylinder Sharpie locomotive at its head. A rake of early four-wheel stock, with a carriage truck at the rear. From the LSWR guide of 1845. *John Scott-Morgan collection*

Left:
The LSWR branch to Windsor, showing the line from Datchet near the terminus in Windsor. From the LSWR guide of 1845. *John Scott-Morgan collection*

Adams 4-4-0 No 445 approaches Earlsfield with a southbound express *c*1889. An interesting photograph showing the timber signalbox, with early contractor-style lettering, and providing a good view of the wooden-posted lower-quadrant signals. *R. C. Stumpf collection*

Late 19th century, 1881-1900

Adams radial tank No 51 heads a local train from Southampton into Totton & Eling in the late 1880s. The station, in its LSWR colour scheme of salmon pink and brown, is shown to good effect. *Lens of Sutton collection*

An Adams small 4-4-0 heads a passenger train into the platform at Woolston station *c*1889. Unlike some of the later, timber structures, this station has a stone-and-brick main building not unlike the earlier London & Southampton style. *Lens of Sutton collection*

'Jubilee' Class A12 0-4-2 tender locomotive No 552 stands at Eastleigh station in the early 1890s with a train of Panter non-corridor bogie stock. Note the six-wheeler van with 'birdcage' roof at the front of the train. *R. C. Stumpf collection*

Adams radial 4-4-2T No 427 heads a train of four- and six-wheeler stock near Stockbridge *c*1890. This locomotive was built by Robert Stephenson in 1883. *Ian Allan Library*

Adams 'X6' 4-4-0 No 658 leaves Basingstoke for London in 1908; note the Great Western station on the right. The 'X6s' were fitted with 6ft 7in driving wheels; this example was built in 1895 at Nine Elms Works. *Ian Allan Library*

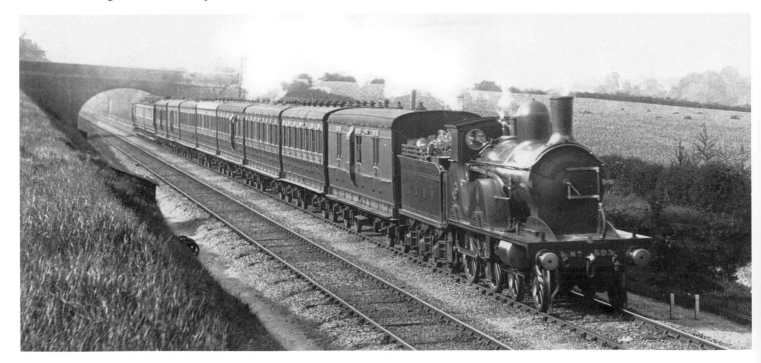

Adams 'X2' 4-4-0 No 593 heads a Portsmouth–Weymouth train near Shawford Junction *c*1899. The carriages at the rear are through coaches from Birkenhead. *Ian Allan Library*

The station at Dean *c*1886, with a stopping service waiting in the platform. The signalbox is of interest as an example of early LSWR design with outside framing. On the right is the stationmaster's house.
Lens of Sutton collection

Bournemouth *c*1898, with an westbound express departing behind Beattie 4-4-0 No 0353, rebuilt by Adams in 1890. These early 4-4-0s had 6ft 7in driving wheels and were originally designed to burn coke. After rebuilding and re-boilering they became useful mixed-traffic locomotives. This is a good view of the west end of Bournemouth station, with its substantial brick signalbox and lattice signals.
E. W. Fry

Adams '460' class 4-4-0 No 474 with a Weymouth–Bournemouth service *c*1898. The class had 6ft 7in driving wheels. This example has a Drummond chimney.
John Scott-Morgan collection

Left:
An interior view of Bournemouth station *c*1899, showing the overall roof and the track layout with its centre carriage roads, as crowds of late-Victorian sea- and sun-worshippers return from their annual holiday. *Lens of Sutton collection*

Right:
Adams '460' class 4-4-0 No 136 heads a special train of Panter six-wheeler stock, built by Beyer Peacock in 1880. These versatile 4-4-0s remained in service with the Southern Railway until the early 1930s, mostly in the West Country.
Ian Allan Library

Left:
A further view of Basingstoke, looking south, with the overall roof of the Great Western station on the right and on the left the original LSWR station, which was later rebuilt in the early 20th century, at the time of the quadrupling from London.
Lens of Sutton collection

Below right:
'T6' 4-4-0 No 686 heads an up local train near Haslemere *c*1900. Note the driver (on the front of the locomotive) checking the smokebox door and lubricants — a practice full of danger that even then was frowned upon and entailed balancing along the side of the locomotive from the cab to the front running-plate. The train has an interesting formation, with two vans leading.
Ian Allan Library

Left:
A mixed freight, headed by Beyer Peacock outside-framed goods 0-6-0 No 287 and consisting of mixed open wagons, with road brake van at both ends, that at the far end being a four-wheeled full-brake parcels van. *John Scott-Morgan collection*

Ashtead station, on the joint LBSCR/LSWR line from Epsom, *c*1890s, showing the timber buildings and the signalbox with its brick base and timber top. *R. C. Stumpf collection*

The outside of Godalming station *c*1899, showing the substantial stone building of distinctive style. Godalming was at the head of the main line to Havant, known as the Portsmouth Direct, built by Thomas Brassey as a speculative venture and later purchased by the LSWR. *Lens of Sutton collection*

Right:
Adams 'T6' 4-4-0 No 685, built at Nine Elms in 1892, speeds a southbound Bournemouth express through Woking *c*1900. This was the second Woking station, the first being Woking Common, built to a style not unlike that at Micheldever. The long line of buildings on the left is a street of shops that still stand today. *Ian Allan Library*

Left:
The 'London' end of Woking *c*1900, again showing the platform arrangement and also the overall roof on Platform 5. Note the vans and carriage trucks at the far bay platform and the 'WOKING JUNCTION' station signs. *Lens of Sutton collection*

Below:
A Class A12 'Jubilee' 0-4-2 races south towards Brookwood with a semi-fast train *c*1900. This picture shows the extensive sidings at the west end of Woking station, at this time full of assorted carriage stock and (in the far distance) carriage trucks.
R. C. Stumpf collection

Left:
Drummond 'T9' 4-4-0 No 711, built by Dübs in 1899, heads a train south near Haslemere *c*1900. The 'T9s' were probably the most successful and famous of the locomotives designed by Dugald Drummond and were later rebuilt by Robert Urie. *Ian Allan Library*

Below:
South Western in the snow. Salisbury in the last years of the 19th century, with two snowed-in Adams 4-4-0s, that on the left being prototype No 460.
R. C. Stumpf collection

A Drummond steam railcar arrives at Andover Town station *c*1910 with a service from Andover Junction. This line connected the main LSWR West of England line with Southampton via Romsey and was once an important cross-country route.
R. C. Stumpf collection

Right:
A Drummond '700' class 0-6-0 goods heads a Class A goods south near Mortlake *c*1915. This train has an interesting make-up of wagons, from a variety of railways. The composition of these goods trains was quite fascinating, often featuring wagons from pre-Grouping railways from as far away as Scotland and the North of England. *Ian Allan Library*

Below:
A panoramic view, facing south, of Clapham Junction *c*1907/8. An Adams 4-4-0 heads towards Waterloo with an up express while an 'M7' 0-4-4T waits with an up local from the Hounslow loop, also for Waterloo. The overall-gantry signalboxes were a feature of Clapham Junction for over 70 years. *Ian Allan Library*

The Edwardian era, 1901-1910

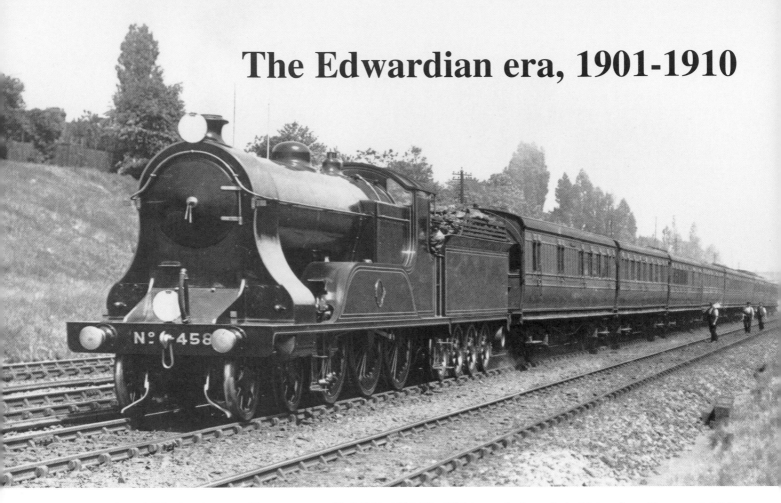

'T14' 4-6-0 No 458 hauls a down corridor express near Earlsfield *c*1910. The 'T14s' were the best of a bad lot, as far as Drummond 4-6-0s are concerned. Drummond seems to have had a problem with thermodynamics, almost to the point where (unlike Churchward on the Great Western) he thought that all that was necessary to make a good 4-6-0 was to put an extra ring in the boiler barrel. The result had to be seen to be believed! *R. C. Stumpf collection*

Above:
Two fine examples of Adams 4-4-0s at their best, the leading locomotive being a 'T3' No 574 and the second 'X6' No 659, at Clapham yard *c*1906. The locomotives are in full Drummond lined green but are still in original mechanical condition.
R. C. Stumpf collection

Right:
Drummond 'K10' 'Small Hopper' 4-4-0 No 383 enters Clapham Junction station from the Waterloo direction *c*1904. The train has a headcode for Waterloo Nine Elms goods yard; perhaps the working entailed a fast run to Clapham Junction and then a tender-first working back to Nine Elms. The vans in the far right are LBSCR milk vans. *John Scott-Morgan collection*

Below left:
Clapham Junction, looking towards London *c*1907/8, with a Drummond 4-6-0 on a down express passing an up express. On the far left a suburban train, with locomotive running bunker-first, makes for Clapham from Addison Road, Kensington, while in the centre a second suburban train heads north to Waterloo. On the right is a Brighton-line service for Victoria.
R. C. Stumpf collection

No 457, a Drummond 'G14' 4-6-0 built at Nine Elms Works in 1908, heads an up express near Earlsfield c1909. The train, of Surrey Warner stock, includes a dining car with a clerestory roof; these vehicles would be rebuilt by the Southern Railway in the 1930s. *Ian Allan Library*

Above left:
Class L12 4-4-0 No 432, built at Nine Elms Works in 1905, passes Earlsfield with a down corridor express c1908. The practice of marshalling a loose non-corridor composite carriage next to the locomotive was then commonplace as a way of strengthening trains consisting of fixed sets. *Ian Allan Library*

Left:
Class T9 4-4-0 No 303 heads a Bournemouth train of Panter non-corridor bogie stock, with a Surrey Warner bogie corridor Brake leading, between Clapham Cutting and Earlsfield c1910. *Ian Allan Library*

Class T9 4-4-0 No 716 near New Malden c1908, with a down corridor express. The locomotive has a Drummond cross-tube firebox and 'water cart' tender. *R. C. Stumpf collection*

Above:
The reconstructed Basingstoke station *c*1910, looking towards London and showing the Alton bay platform on the far right.
Ian Allan Library

Above:
Class G14 4-6-0 No 457 with a down
express of corridor stock at Wilton *c*1910.
No 457 was built at Nine Elms in 1908.
In later years these locomotives would be
relegated to goods-train diagrams.
Ian Allan Library

Below left:
Near Overton in 1909, Class T14 4-6-0
No 443 heads a North Cornwall express
formed of Panter non-corridor stock.
John Scott-Morgan collection

Class P14 4-6-0 No 449 heads a dining-car express towards the West of England *c*1911.
This locomotive was built at Eastleigh in 1910 and would be withdrawn by the Southern
Railway in 1927. *R. C. Stumpf collection*

Above:
A general view of Yeovil Junction *c*1910, showing a wide variety of wagons from the LSWR and other pre-Grouping railways, including a pair of covered vans and a brake van. *Lens of Sutton collection*

Another view of a Drummond steam railcar, this time at Bournemouth Central *c*1908, showing the cluttered platforms with luggage, bookstalls and barrows all along the far platform. This building, with its overall roof, has recently been restored. *Lens of Sutton collection*

Left:
Botley station, facing Eastleigh, *c*1909, with a Drummond steam railcar on the Bishops Waltham branch service.
Lens of Sutton collection

Derailed 'L12' No 422 receiving attention from the breakdown gang at Bournemouth *c*1912. The rear driving wheels will require jacking and packing in order to re-rail the locomotive. *Lens of Sutton collection*

33

The last years, 1911-1922

Left:
Drummond Class E10 'Double Single' No 373 heads a train of Panter non-corridor stock through Clapham Cutting on a Salisbury express *c*1920. *R. C. Stumpf collection*

Below left:
Urie-rebuilt 'L12' 4-4-0 No 417 hauls a Bournemouth express formed of mixed bogie stock near Earlsfield *c*1920. Note the three-car electric train to the (distant) right. *R. C. Stumpf collection*

Above right:
Urie-rebuilt 'T14' 4-6-0 No 447 near Earlsfield *c*1922 with a down Bournemouth express of non-corridor stock.
The locomotive was built at Eastleigh in June 1911 and rebuilt at Eastleigh in 1917. *Ian Allan Library*

Centre right:
Drummond 'K10' 4-4-0 No 152, built at Nine Elms in 1902, hauls a train of Panter non-corridor stock on a down train near Earlsfield *c*1922. *Ian Allan Library*

Below:
Sister locomotive No 137 speeds through Clapham Cutting with a down train of mixed non-corridor bogie stock *c*1922. *Ian Allan Library*

Above left:
Urie 'H15' 4-6-0 No 489 with an express near Earlsfield *c*1920. The locomotive was built at Eastleigh Works in 1914.
Ian Allan Library

Below left:
Sister 'H15' 4-6-0 No 482, also built at Eastleigh in 1914, speeds through Earlsfield station with a down express *c*1921. These locomotives had 6ft driving wheels. *Ian Allan Library*

Above:
Class T9 4-4-0 No 284, built at Nine Elms in 1899, in rebuilt form with superheated boiler at Esher *c*1922 with a down express of Panter non-corridor stock.
Ian Allan Library

Centre right:
Two Adams 4-4-0s take a down train through Esher *c*1920. The leading locomotive is No 581, a Class X2 with 7ft 1in driving wheels, and has been modified with Drummond fittings, including chimney; the second locomotive is Class T6 No 685 in largely original condition, with stovepipe chimney.
Ian Allan Library

Right:
Class L12 4-4-0 No 424 heads a semi-fast away from Weybridge on 7 August 1911. This locomotive has a Drummond water-tube firebox, as originally built. These fireboxes were not very successful, as they required a lot of maintenance.
R. C. Stumpf collection

Rebuilt 'T14' 4-6-0 No 444 leaves
Basingstoke with a fast to London in July
1920. The line of wagons on the far left
is made up of horseboxes. *P. Rutherford*

Class A12 'Jubilee' 0-4-2 No 537 with a
pick-up goods train consisting of wagons
from a wide variety of pre-Grouping
railways, including the North Eastern
and the Great Western.
Historical Model Railway Society

An aerial view of Portsmouth & Southsea
station in the late 1920s, showing the line
south to Portsmouth Harbour, the terminal
platforms (far left) and the goods depot
(right foreground). *R. C. Stumpf collection*

A general view of the new Feltham Yard c1922, with Urie 'G16' 4-8-0T No 495, built at Eastleigh in 1921. Feltham Yard was one of the LSWR's most important projects in the post-World War 1 era, serving South West London and providing both the LSWR and later the Southern Railway with a modern facility to sort freight for cross-London traffic. This was done over a series of humps, and the 'G16s', with 5ft 1in driving wheels, were designed specifically for this work. *Ian Allan Library*

Urie 'S15' 4-6-0 No 505 at Feltham Yard c1922 with a heavy freight train of open wagons and vans. These powerful 4-6-0s were designed to handle heavy freight traffic on the LSWR and survived on this work until 1964. Fortunately, two members of the class are still with us, Nos 499 and 506 both being owned by the Urie Locomotive Society. *R. C. Stumpf collection*

An interesting view of Yeovil Town c1919, showing the overall station roofs and extensive yard, with a variety of Drummond and Adams locomotives on shed. Yeovil also had two other stations, the others being the GWR's Yeovil Pen Mill and Yeovil Junction, on the LSWR main line to Exeter. *R. Blencowe collection*

An Edwardian view of Chard Junction with a gathering of passengers on the down platform to the left. Advertisements adorn the building on the up platform including Maple & Co and Players Navy Cut cigarettes. *Ian Allan Library*

Left:
Class T14 4-6-0 No 446 climbs Honiton Bank with a heavy passenger train from Waterloo to Exeter in July 1913. *R. C. Stumpf collection*

Right:
In the last months of the LSWR, Urie 'N15' 4-6-0 No 747, built at Eastleigh in 1922, arrives at Exeter with a down Plymouth express formed of Surrey Warner corridor bogie stock. The wagons in the background (left) are of interest, with a variety of private-owner wagons in the yard. *Ian Allan Library*

Left:
Class L12 4-4-0 No 433 heads a fast express of various vans and non-corridor passenger stock near Sidmouth Junction in July 1913.
R. C. Stumpf collection

Above:
Drummond 'L11' 4-4-0 No 173 with a freight near Whimple c1912. This picture shows the locomotive in original condition, with cross-tube firebox (later removed) and six-wheel tender (later replaced by an eight-wheel 'water cart'). The leading wagon is an LSWR van, followed by a train of five- and eight-plank wagons.
R. C. Stumpf collection

Above:
Class T9 4-4-0 No 722 departs Waterloo with a train of Panter bogie stock *c*1900. At this time Waterloo was a hotch-potch of add-on buildings dating from 1848 right through to the 1880s. The need to rebuild the station became more urgent as the early years of the 20th century went by, until it was decided that two thirds of the station should be completely replaced, to improve facilities and train operations. *Lens of Sutton collection*

Below:
Waterloo 'A' 'box *c*1890s, showing the gantry 'box which straddled the main line until the 1930s, when the Southern Railway replaced it with a new concrete-and-steel reinforced structure. Note the tall signals on brackets (which required many thousands of yards of steel cable to operate) and also the signal controlling entry to and exit from the station. *John Scott-Morgan collection*

Waterloo

Right:
Drummond 'P14' 4-6-0 No 452 at Waterloo at the head of Surrey Warner corridor stock *c*1913. Comparison with the previous photograph shows the progress being made with the new overall station roof, over Platforms 1-4. *Ian Allan Library*

The first Drummond 'F13' 4-6-0, No 330, at Waterloo when new in 1905. The 'F13s' had 6ft driving wheels and a water-tube firebox and would have found it hard to pull the skin off an Edwardian rice pudding. Even when No 330 was rebuilt by Robert Urie during World War 1, the locomotive left a lot to be desired. *Ian Allan Library*

Right:
A hive of activity in the cab road at the old Waterloo *c*1900, with a selection of Hansom cabs and Hackney carriages awaiting custom. *Lens of Sutton collection*

Above right:
A second view of Waterloo in 1910, with a close-up of the platforms that are yet to be rebuilt, showing the so-called 'native village' of odd buildings (far distance) and the 1850s and 1860s buildings to be replaced with higher overall roof. A suburban train stands at Platform 2 and an up express has arrived at Platform 5, both behind Drummond locomotives. *Ian Allan Library*

Below right:
On the same day on Platform 2, a local train is about to depart headed by two Adams 'T1' 0-4-4Ts, whilst in the background a dining-car express stands at Platform 5. This picture affords a good view of the new roof and the luggage lifts with the offices in the distance — features that fortunately are still with us. *Ian Allan Library*

Above:
Rush hour on the Windsor platforms in Edwardian times. A Drummond '700' class 0-6-0 has arrived with a train of six-wheel stock full of commuters heading for city offices in their bowlers, straw hats and cloth caps. *Lens of Sutton collection*

Right:
Platforms 1-5 at the new Waterloo *c*1910, showing the new light, airy, open station, in contrast to the old dark, dingy, cramped structure, with its labyrinth of odd buildings. This is the rush hour, before electric trains were introduced at these platforms in 1915. *R. C. Stumpf collection*

A Class E10 'Double Single' at the buffer stops after bringing in an up train. This photograph, taken *c*1902, shows the old overall roof with its iron-column construction, later replaced by the new structure in steel and glass. *Ian Allan Library*

Class T14 departure, with No 446 heading its train of non-corridor stock out of the station. The backdrop of the mighty overall roof makes for a dramatic sight, whilst an 'M7' 0-4-4T waits in the siding for its next local service. *Ken Nunn collection / LCGB*

Class L11 4-4-0 No 440 departs Waterloo with a semi-fast *c*1922. Built at Nine Elms in 1907, the locomotive has been dual-fitted with Westinghouse air brake and has had its water-tube firebox removed.
Ian Allan Library

Class T9 4-4-0 No 310 leaves Waterloo with a Southampton express *c*1922. The locomotive has had its firebox changed but has yet to have its boiler replaced by a Urie example. *A. W. V. Mace*

New-look station and new-look locomotive. Urie 'N15' 4-6-0 No 744 at Waterloo in early Southern days (1924). The Urie 4-6-0s of the 'N15' and 'S15' classes represented the company's last look forward and were a fine way to see out the old company. *R. C. Stumpf collection*

London suburban

Left:
Putney station *c*1912 on the line from
Wandsworth to Wimbledon, which became
joint with the District Railway and was the
first suburban line on the LSWR to be
electrified, in 1915. This interesting
photograph shows a period of transition,
with horse buses and new LGOC B-type
motor buses outside the station.
R. C. Stumpf collection

Below left:
East Putney station, *c*1903, with a District
train of four-wheeler stock headed by a
Beyer Peacock 4-4-0T. This station was
served by LSWR trains to Waterloo via
Clapham Junction and District trains to
Mansion House via Earls Court.
R. C. Stumpf collection

Turnham Green *c*1900, showing the original station with its two platforms before the
quadrupling a few years later. At this time the LSWR and the District ran joint services to
Richmond through this station. By 1912 the line had been rebuilt to take four tracks,
which accommodated services to Richmond (LSWR and District), to Ealing Broadway
and South Harrow (District) and to Hounslow Barracks (District). The LSWR route ran
via Addison Road and Hammersmith. The LSWR ceased to run trains over this line in
1916. *Lens of Sutton collection*

Gunnersbury station *c*1906, a year after the District electrified, showing an Adams radial 4-4-2T with a train for Richmond in the platform.
This was the next station south from Turnham Green and was served by the LSWR, District and North London railways, the platform
on the far left (without an awning) being for the North London Railway. Note the fine array of lattice-posted signals at both ends of the
station. *R. C. Stumpf collection*

Richmond station *c*1900, showing the old LSWR Station Hotel, which would be rebuilt in Southern days. A 'T1' 0-4-4T waits with a train of six-wheeler stock as an Adams Radial 4-4-2T running bunker-first hauls its train out of the station. *Lens of Sutton collection*

The Urie-reboilered 'M7' 0-4-4T, No 126, with a mixed train of bogie stock runs through Clapham Cutting *c*1922. This locomotive was rebuilt in June 1921 but, unlike so many rebuilds of Drummond locomotives by Robert Urie, was not a success, being heavier than the original specification. This meant that the locomotive could be used only on certain lines and did not have the route availability of its sisters. No 126 nevertheless survived into Southern days and was not withdrawn until it broke a crank axle at Guildford London Road station in May 1937. *John Scott-Morgan collection*

An Adams Radial 4-4-2T runs bunker-first through Clapham Cutting *c*1916, just prior to the electrification of LSWR suburban services to Hampton Court. The train is heading for Waterloo and is composed of bogie non-corridor stock. In the distance can be seen the newly built power station at Durnsford Road which generated the power for the system. *Ian Allan Library*

An 'M7' 0-4-4T and train of bogie stock cross the bridge at Earlsfield station *c*1909. It was the electric trams, evidence of which can be seen here, that convinced the LSWR to electrify its suburban network. *R. C. Stumpf collection*

Class O2 0-4-4T No 196 at Weybridge with an outer-suburban train on 28 April 1921. No 196 was built at Nine Elms Works in 1891 and represented one of the finest tank classes ever to run on the LSWR. Members of this class later went to the Isle of Wight, where they were well received and lasted in traffic until December 1966. Note the non-corridor bogie stock in salmon pink and brown. *H. C. Casserley*

Above left:
A busy scene at Coombe & Malden station *c*1905, with city folk about to join a cramped train of four-wheeler stock for London, headed by an Adams Radial 4-4-2T. *Lens of Sutton collection*

Left:
Surbiton station (the original Kingston when first opened) *c*1910. Locomotive Superintendent Dugald Drummond lived a few hundred yards from this station, and it was from here that he made his journey each morning to either Nine Elms or Eastleigh, in the 4-2-4T, 'The Bug'. *R. C. Stumpf collection*

A Radial tank speeds a commuter train on the Kingston loop *c*1915. Note the conductor rail in place for the imminent electrification, and the suburban houses with allotments close to the track. *R. C. Stumpf collection*

Hampton Wick *c*1905, showing the station and signalbox. The platforms and buildings are neat and well kept, and the paintwork in a fresh state. Note the station staff taking a short cut across the main line — a practice frowned upon even then. *R. C. Stumpf collection*

An 'M7' 0-4-4T simmers at Windsor station *c*1910 with a bogie train for Waterloo. This fine overall-roof station is still standing and has been restored in recent years. *R. C. Stumpf collection*

Above right:
Bracknell station, on the line to Reading via Virginia Water and Egham, *c*1910. The signalbox is in original condition, with external framework; many of these 'boxes were later boarded in. *R. C. Stumpf collection*

Right:
Camberley station, on the line from Ascot to Ash Vale, *c*1900, facing Ascot, with the staff dressed in their best for a photograph. This attractive station was destroyed in the 1960s and replaced with a concrete monstrosity, at a time when British Rail had no respect for its heritage. Note the timber signalbox and gates in the middle distance. *Ian Allan Library*

The Bodmin & Wadebridge Railway

Above left:
Fletcher Jennings 0-4-0ST *Bodmin*, built in 1864, heads a train of early four-wheeler carriage stock at Wadebridge *c*1875. The second vehicle (thought to be of original London & Southampton origin) and the Open next to the brake van have survived to be preserved in the National Collection at York. *R. C. Stumpf collection*

Below left:
Activity at Bodmin *c*1875, with wagons awaiting unloading next to the goods sheds and a train of three-plank open wagons full of coal. *Ian Allan Library*

Above:
The Bodmin & Wadebridge First and Second Class carriage, left, in its blue and cream livery, coupled to the Third class open carriage, right. Both these carriages were exhibited on the concourse of Waterloo station for many years before being sent to the old York Railway Museum. They are now on exhibition at the present York Museum. They are seen at Waterloo siding shortly after being restored, in the background is a trian of Pantcr arc roof stock.
Ian Allan Library

Below:
The Fletcher Jennings 0-4-0ST *Bodmin* as new in 1864 before delivery to the line. *Ian Allan Library*

Exeter, North Devon and Cornwall

Above left:
Exeter Queen Street *c*1913, looking towards Exmouth Junction. The extensive goods yard and carriage sidings are filled with a variety of wagons from a large number of pre-Grouping railways and rakes of Panter bogie carriage stock. *Ian Allan Library*

Below left:
Queen Street again, this time looking towards St Davids, showing a group of locomotives waiting to take their trains on to London or more local locations. From left to right are 'T9' 4-4-0 No 727, 'T3' 4-4-0 No 576 and an unidentified 'A12' 'Jubilee' 0-4-2. Queen Street would become Central following rebuilding in Southern days. *Ian Allan Library*

Top right:
Adams 4-4-0 No 380 at Queen Street in 1904 on a transfer freight to the Great Western. Note the five-plank open wagon full of hay. *Roger Carpenter collection*

Centre right:
An 'O2' 0-4-4T running bunker-first skirts the Exe near Lympstone station *c*1912 with a local train of six-wheeler stock on the Exmouth branch. *Ian Allan Library*

Right:
Lympstone station *c*1900, showing the basic brick-and-timber station building with its cement facing. The buildings sport a whole plethora of adverts and railway poster-boards. *John Scott-Morgan collection*

Left:
Eggesford, on the North Devon line, with station staff posing for the camera *c*1890. This is a good example of a station built of local materials, in this case with cement rendering. *Lens of Sutton collection*

Below left:
Barnstaple Junction *c*1905, looking towards Exeter. The station buildings on this line were built of local stone, as seen here. Note the yard full of wagons and the carriage stock ready for marshalling for use on local services. *Lens of Sutton collection*

'M7' 0-4-4T No 22 departs Ilfracombe station with a service for Barnstaple Junction *c*1912. This station stood above the town, entailing a steep, hilly walk for any prospective passenger. The carriage sidings are full of LSWR and Great Western bogie stock. *Ian Allan Library*

A Urie-rebuilt 'T9' 4-4-0 heads a dining-car express out of Okehampton *c*1920. Okehampton was one of the most important stations in North Devon, with services to London, Exeter, Plymouth, Bude and Padstow. *Ken Nunn collection / LCGB*

Meldon Viaduct c1925. This impressive structure was, not far from Meldon Quarry, which supplied the LSWR with most of its track ballast and also raw material to make concrete products at Exmouth Works. The viaduct was originally built as a single-line structure, but later a second viaduct was built alongside to make it double-track. *Ken Nunn collection / LCGB*

An 'O2' 0-4-4T arrives at Bere Alston with a local stopping train for Plymouth c1909. This was the junction for the independent Plymouth, Devonport & South Western Junction Railway, which ran from here to Callington. *Lens of Sutton collection*

Adams 'X6' 4-4-0 No 660, built at Nine Elms in 1895, speeds an up express through Lipson Junction (near Plymouth) in the early years of the 20th century. It was at this point that the LSWR and the Great Western ran over joint lines to Plymouth. The LSWR reached Plymouth over the lines owned by the Plymouth, Devonport & South Western Junction Railway, which did not become part of the LSWR until 1922. *Ian Allan Library*

The outside of Bude station *c*1900, showing the stone-built station building. A train stands at the platform while a group of horse-drawn road vehicles await passengers. *Ian Allan Library*

'X6' 4-4-0 No 657 stands at the head of a local train at Bude *c*1920. As express trains became heavier, the older Adams 4-4-0s were sent westward to the lines west of Exeter to work the local services, many lasting into the late 1920s and early 1930s on these duties. *Ken Nunn collection / LCGB*

Above left:
Bodmin station *c*1914, with a single Panter arch-roof bogie Brake Third at the platform. The goods yard is full of open coal wagons, but the platform is strangely empty of passengers. *Ian Allan Library*

Left:
The other end of the branch at Wadebridge *c*1913, looking towards Padstow and showing the substantial timber footbridge adjacent to a timber-and-brick station building. In the distance a Drummond steam railcar can be seen approaching on a local service. *Ian Allan Library*

Above:
One of the three long-lasting Beattie 2-4-0 well tanks, No 0314, rounds the curve near Padstow with a single-bogie Brake Third carriage. The three 2-4-0WTs were retained in order to work the Bodmin-Wenford Bridge line, which had sharp curves, but also worked local services to Padstow from Wadebridge, as seen in this photograph taken in 1921. *Ian Allan Library*

Calstock, on the Plymouth, Devonport & South Western Junction Railway, on the opening day, 2 March 1908, with crowds on the platform awaiting the first official train. *Lens of Sutton collection*

The Plymouth, Devonport & South Western Junction Railway

A few days earlier, Hawthorn 0-6-0T *A. S. Harris* in Oxford blue poses at Gunnislake station. Note the road delivery wagon and the wagons on the goods train lettered 'PD&SW'. This railway had a very close and cordial relationship with the LSWR, which used its lines from Bere Alston to the outskirts of Plymouth. *Lens of Sutton collection*

Calstock station and viaduct *c*1910. This viaduct, which crosses the Tamar, is still in use on the branch, which now runs as far as Gunnislake, the Callington section having closed in 1966. *Lens of Sutton collection*

The Lynton & Barnstaple Railway

Above:
The 1ft 11½in-gauge Lynton & Barnstaple Railway was built as an independent light railway in the late 1890s and was not taken over by the LSWR until 1922, in anticipation of the Grouping in 1923. Manning Wardle 2-6-2T *Taw* simmers at Lynton & Lynmouth station *c*1912 with a train of passenger bogie stock for Barnstaple. *John Scott-Morgan collection*

Right:
Lyn at Pilton locomotive shed *c*1922. This Baldwin 2-4-2T was built in Philadelphia in 1898 during the great locomotive famine (when British builders had full order books and were unable to oblige) and, until the purchase of the USA dock tanks in 1946, was the only American locomotive on the Southern Railway. Note the Adams stovepipe chimney, fitted when the locomotive went to Eastleigh for an overhaul. *John Scott-Morgan collection*

The Somerset & Dorset
and associated lines

Above:
The Somerset & Dorset Joint Railway was owned jointly by the LSWR and the Midland Railway, the former being responsible for infrastructure and the latter for locomotives and rolling stock, but to a great extent it had an identity of its own, with its Prussian-blue livery for locomotives and carriage stock. Here, *c*1914, a Midland-type Avonside 0-4-4T crosses the Great Western main line at Highbridge, with a van train from the harbour. Note the LSWR-designed signalbox and footbridge.
Lens of Sutton collection

Left:
Radstock *c*1910, with a train arriving at the station with a 4-4-0 at its head. Radstock was very important to the S&D, as this part of the line served a number of local coal mines, which produced much lucrative traffic. *Lens of Sutton collection*

Above:
A very tranquil and peaceful scene at Spetisbury station on 15 July 1893 as an 0-4-4T, No 10, arrives with a local passenger train, the 4.13pm from Templecombe. Note the disc-and-bar signal and the passenger with straw boater. *T. F. Budden*

Below:
Templecombe station *c*1900, with 0-6-0 goods No 35 at the head of a passenger train. Note the number of vans and full-brake parcels vans that seem to populate the adjacent siding at the back of the station, used mostly for milk traffic. *Lens of Sutton collection*

The Isle of Wight

The LSWR and the LBSCR had a joint interest in the railway from Ryde Pier Head to Ryde St Johns Road station. This view, taken in early Southern days (c1927), shows the line at Ryde Pier Head, with an electric tram on the pier tramway during the period before the Drewry railcars were introduced. The three-arm bracket signal in the foreground is of LBSCR origin. *Ian Allan Library*

Ryde Esplanade station c1910, with an Isle of Wight Railway Beyer Peacock 2-4-0T and a train of four-wheel stock awaiting the road to Ventnor. This picture shows the whole pier and Ryde Pier Head station, terminus for the ferry service to Portsmouth. *R. C. Stumpf collection*

LSWR 'O2' 0-4-4T No 211 heads a train of Isle of Wight Railway four-wheel stock near Wroxall c1923, shortly after its transfer to the island for evaluation trials, along with sister locomotive No 206. These were the first of 19 members of the class to be shipped across to the island for a further lease of life after the London-suburban electrification. *R. C. Stumpf collection*

Above:
Ryde St Johns Road station, looking towards Ryde Esplanade, *c*1924. This picture shows the Isle of Wight Railway works to the right, with the main repair shops and a wind-powered water pump in the background. In the foreground (right) is a train of ex-North London Railway four-wheelers. The platforms are built of timber, later replaced with brick. Note the ornate gas lamps. *Ian Allan Library*

Below:
Ryde St Johns Road station again, this time facing south, showing the signalbox (ex-SECR from Waterloo Junction) and the lower-quadrant signals at the end of the platforms. *Ian Allan Library*

The Midland & South Western Junction Railway had a long and close relationship with the LSWR, operating a line from Andover through Swindon Town to Andoversford and Cheltenham Lansdown. Here an MSWJR 2-4-0 tender locomotive, resplendent in Midland crimson lake, arrives at Andover with a train of LSWR corridor stock, probably a through train to Southampton, c1910. *Ian Allan Library*

Associated minor and joint railways

The Lee-on-Solent Light Railway was operated by the LSWR on behalf of the light-railway company; it was never owned by the LSWR and always ran at a loss for its owners. Manning Wardle 0-6-0ST No 459, purchased by the LSWR in March 1884 from a contractor for engineers' use, simmers at Fort Brockhurst c1910. *Ian Allan Library*

The Brookwood Necropolis Railway was built in the middle decades of the 19th century to serve Brookwood cemetery, one of the largest in Britain, owned by the London Necropolis Company. A regular train service from the company's private station at Waterloo operated until the latter's destruction during the Blitz of 1940, whereafter all services between Waterloo and Brookwood were suspended. This picture was taken in the early 1930s at the Brookwood end of the line. *John Scott-Morgan collection*

The LSWR served a number of military establishments within its extensive network and had a long connection with the Army. During World War 1 Hudswell Clarke 0-6-0ST *Hampshire* poses with a group of khaki-clad soldiers at Fovant, Wiltshire, on the Fovant Camp Railway. The train behind the locomotive is made up of four non-corridor bogie carriages, probably on a through service from Waterloo to the camp railway. *John Scott-Morgan collection*

The LSWR and the Army

The LSWR provided trains for the military, both in peacetime and war. Here we see a company of the Royal Engineers detraining for their summer camp somewhere on Salisbury Plain in 1911. *Lens of Sutton collection*

War Department Beyer Peacock 2-4-0T No 94 (ex-MSWJR No 8) at Longmoor Camp c1915, with a group of sappers posing for the photographer. The Woolmer Instructional Military Railway ran from a terminus at Liss to Longmoor Camp in Hampshire; a further branch ran up to Bordon to connect with the LSWR branch terminus there. Opened at the beginning of the 20th century, it was used to train many thousands of sappers for both World Wars and survived until 1971. *R. Carpenter / Coutanche collection*

The last new lines

Above:
West Meon on the Meon Valley line, opened to traffic in 1903. This rare photograph shows the earthworks newly built and finished and the station in its first coat of paint, just after opening in 1903.
Lens of Sutton collection

Above:
West Meon again, probably on the same day, with a platelayers' gang at work tiding the ballast in the station platform; the stations on the Meon Valley were very substantial for a rural link line. Running from Alton to Fareham through some sparsely populated areas, the line closed to passengers in 1955 and goods in the late 1960s, by which time only a stub-end in both directions was in use.
Lens of Sutton collection

Herriard station on the Basingstoke & Alton Light Railway, which opened to traffic in 1900. The station buildings, made of timber and corrugated iron, stood on concrete-faced platforms — a by-product of the stone dust from Meldon Quarry. The line closed during World War 1 but had to be reinstated after the war, only to close again in 1936. *R. C. Stumpf collection*

Bentworth & Lasham station *c*1901, shortly after opening, with part of the village in the background. Both the Meon Valley and the Basingstoke & Alton were 'blocking' lines, to keep out the Great Western. *R. C. Stumpf collection*

Locomotives

'Mazeppa' class 2-2-2 tender locomotive No 57 *Meteor*, designed by C. V. Gooch and built at Nine Elms Works in 1847. The 10 members of this class represented contemporary locomotive design at its best. *Meteor* was withdrawn and broken up in 1862. *Ian Allan Library*

Beattie 0-6-0 goods No 8, formerly named *Vesta*, built at Nine Elms in 1870 but later rebuilt with a new cab and chimney. *Ian Allan Library*

Above.
No 0365, one of W. G. Beattie's '348' class 4-4-0s, which were a disaster as built and shown here. Built in 1877 by Sharp Stewart, some were later rebuilt successfully by Adams, although No 0365 was not one of these. The *débâcle* over these locomotives would lead to Beattie's early departure from the LSWR. *Ian Allan Library*

Below:
Adams rebuilt the '348' class after he took office in January 1878. No 351 is seen at Exmouth in 1892 in early Adams pea-green livery and with stovepipe chimney. *Ian Allan Library*

Class A12 'Jubilee' 0-4-2 tender locomotive No 539 in early condition with Beattie tender and stovepipe chimney. Built in 1888 and not withdrawn until September 1930, the 'A12s' were some of the best express locomotives built by the company. The type's 'Jubilee' nickname arose from Queen Victoria's Golden Jubilee of 1887. *Ian Allan Library*

Class 395 0-6-0 goods No 511, built by Neilson in 1883. These locomotives had long and varied careers, some being sold to the War Department during World War 1 and serving in the Middle East. *Ian Allan Library*

Drummond 'M7' No 126 was rebuilt by Robert Urie at Eastleigh in July 1921 but was not a total success in this form, being the only member of the class so treated. It was originally reclassified 'X14' in rebuilt form. *Ian Allan Library*

The Drummond 'T9' 4-4-0s were some of the best locomotives ever produced for the LSWR. Here, at Nine Elms, No 773 is seen decorated for hauling a special train. The last survivors of this class would not be withdrawn until 1961. No 120 is preserved on the Bluebell Railway. *R. C. Stumpf collection*

Drummond 'E14' 4-6-0 No 335 was built at Nine Elms in 1907 and was the only member of its class. Like the earlier 'F13' 4-6-0s, it was a great disappointment, its high fuel consumption, in particular, giving rise to various nicknames, including 'coal gobbler' and hence 'turkey'. It was rebuilt as an 'H15' 4-6-0 in December 1914. *Ian Allan Library*

Robert Urie's five 'H16' 4-6-2T locomotives were designed in 1921 for freight-transfer work across London from Feltham Yard to Willesden on the LNWR. They lasted in traffic until 1962. No 519 is seen here at Strawberry Hill in 1922. *R. C. Stumpf collection*

Class G16 4-8-0T No 494 was one of four locomotives of its type built at Eastleigh in 1921 for hump shunting at Feltham Yard, although they sometimes escaped these arduous duties to run trip workings along the main line. *Ian Allan Library*

Urie's 'N15' 4-6-0s were introduced in 1918 and were one of the most successful designs of their day, lasting in traffic until the late 1950s. No 737 is seen with an oil tank fitted in its bogie tender, as part of an experiment of 1919. *Ian Allan Library*

The 'S15' 4-6-0s were designed as mixed-traffic locomotives and were introduced in 1920. Like the 'N15s', they were a great success, and the design (with modifications) would be perpetuated by R. E. L. Maunsell, the first CME of the Southern Railway. No 507 is seen at Strawberry Hill shed in October 1921. *Ian Allan Library*

In 1919 18 GCR Robinson 2-8-0s (ROD Type 230) were borrowed by the LSWR for use on heavy freights and were stationed at Strawberry Hill in London and at Salisbury for evaluation. However, in 1921 Robert Urie decided not to pursue the experiment and to build more 'S15s' instead. *R. C. Stumpf collection*

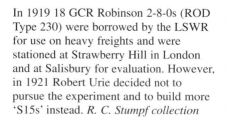

In 1903 the LSWR purchased two LBSCR Class A1 'Terrier' 0-6-0Ts for use on the Lyme Regis branch, which had just opened as a light railway. Originally LBSCR No 46 *Newington*, No 734 would be sold in 1912 to the Freshwater, Yarmouth & Newport Railway on the Isle of Wight. It later became Southern Railway property and eventually British Railways property and is now preserved at Haven Street on the Isle of Wight Steam Railway. *Ian Allan Library*

'The Bug', one of the most famous locomotives designed by Dugald Drummond, built at Nine Elms Works in 1899. With 5ft 7in driving wheels and inspection cab, this 4-2-4T locomotive was used by Drummond to travel all over the LSWR in order to inspect the company's workshops and locomotive depots. It was in almost daily use on this work until 1912, when Drummond died, but his successor Robert Urie did not like it and rarely used it. The intention was to preserve it, but, alas, the Southern Railway broke it up in 1940 for war scrap. It is pictured in store at Eastleigh on 15 April 1922. *Ian Allan Library*

Steam railcars and railmotors

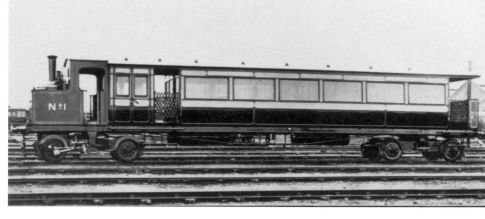

The Southsea branch was owned and operated jointly by the LSWR and the LBSCR. The line was worked by tank locomotives and four- or six-wheel carriage stock until 1903, when Drummond introduced two steam railcars. This is 'K11' No 1 in Eastleigh Works yard in original form with upright boiler; this did not prove successful, and the locomotive was later rebuilt and modified with a horizontal boiler. *R. C. Stumpf collection*

A later view of 'K11' No 1 at Fratton after rebuilding with horizontal boiler following experiments with a second upright boiler. The locomotive portion of the unit was owned by the LSWR, while the carriage portion was owned by the LBSCR! Nos 1 and 2 were both withdrawn shortly before World War 1 and stored, not being broken up until the early 1920s. No 1 had an LSWR-painted 'locomotive' and an LBSCR carriage portion, while No 2 was painted wholly in LSWR livery. *R. C. Stumpf collection*

The second railcar design produced by Drummond was the 'H12', intended for use on branch lines and lightly used suburban services. Nos 1 and 2 were built in 1904 at Nine Elms Works at a cost of £1,380 each; No 1 is seen at Eastleigh c1912. Like the Southsea-branch cars, the 'H12s' suffered from being underpowered and were lacklustre in performance. At first they were used on the Basingstoke & Alton Light Railway, but later both cars were employed on a number of outer-suburban lines, including that from Richmond to Clapham Junction via Kensington Addison Road. Both were withdrawn in the autumn of 1913 and broken up in 1916, after the carriage portions had been converted for motor-train use. *Ian Allan Library*

The 'H13' class railcars were introduced in November 1905 at a cost of £1,475 each. No 5, pictured at Nine Elms Works yard in 1905, was one of the first batch, numbered 3-6. The second batch, Nos 7-15, followed in 1906. These cars had a more pleasing look to them, with the boiler enclosed in the carriage portion. They were not a great success, however, and all except Nos 3, 4 and 10 were withdrawn in 1916 for conversion to motor-trailer carriages; the last three were withdrawn for conversion in July 1919. *Ian Allan Library*

An 'H13' railcar at Hurstbourne c1908, with the driver looking out from the driving compartment. These cars had a hard job hauling themselves along, let alone a trailer as expected by the LSWR Board when they were first introduced. *John Scott-Morgan collection*

Class H13 No 8 at the far end of the LSWR at Bodmin c1912, in the twilight of its career before being withdrawn in October 1916. *Ian Allan Library*

A works photograph of 'C14' 2-2-0 railmotor locomotive No 736. Introduced in September 1906, these small, underpowered locomotives had 3ft driving wheels and were designed to be used on light passenger duties, coupled to 'Gate stock' trailers. They were an unmitigated disaster on this work and were used for a time as light shunters before being offered for sale during World War 1; No 736 was sold to the Ministry of Munitions in 1917, but four members of the class survived to be rebuilt by Robert Urie as 0-4-0Ts for light shunting work. *Ian Allan Library*

By now on the duplicate list, Class C14 2-2-0 No 741 stands at Eastleigh on 1 October 1921. This locomotive was later rebuilt as an 0-4-0T and survived for many years as a shunter in the Southampton area, not being withdrawn until 1957. *Ian Allan Library*

Class C14 2-2-0 No 737 and a train of two 'Gate' trailers at Eastleigh. This photograph belies the fact that these small locomotives could not easily haul two trailers, and the latter quickly found a new role, coupled to motor-fitted 'O2' and 'M7' 0-4-4Ts. *Ian Allan Library*

'S14' 0-4-0T railmotor locomotive No 101 built at the time of the move from Nine Elms to Eastleigh, completed in September 1910. It was intended to build more of these 0-4-0Ts, but the order was cancelled after the boilers for five locomotives had been built, and only two were completed as locomotives, the other three boilers being sold to the War Department for use in military hospitals. Later, in 1917, both 'S14s' would also be sold to the War Department. *Ian Allan Library*

No 42, one of the four sleeping cars ordered in 1907 by Surrey Warner at a cost of £1,400 each for the Plymouth boat-train services. In practice these carriages saw little use with the LSWR and were later sold to the Great Western, the two companies having decided not to race each other with boat-train services from London to Plymouth in the wake of the Salisbury disaster of 1906. *John Scott-Morgan collection*

Carriages

Panter arc-roof bogie non-corridor First No 37 in salmon pink and brown *c*1904. These carriages originally ran in four-car trains but were later used as single carriages tagged on to semi-fast trains. Most were withdrawn in the 1920s and early 1930s. *Lens of Sutton collection*

Pullman parlour car *Duchess of Fife* at Bournemouth Central in July 1901, about to leave on the 2.7pm to Waterloo. These Pullmans, which were of American design, did not last long on the LSWR, which quickly built its own corridor express stock. *Lens of Sutton collection*

Surrey Warner bogie dining carriage No 4139, fitted with later-pattern bogies, at Axminster *c*1922. Note the carriage is painted in late-LSWR sage green. *Lens of Sutton collection*

Surrey Warner bogie family saloon *c*1904. These carriages were also used for invalid traffic. At least one still exists. *Lens of Sutton collection*

At the same time that the sleeping cars were introduced, the LSWR built a number of dining cars for use on the most important services, No 59 being an example. Later, in Southern days, these carriages were rebuilt with elliptical roofs. Two still exist and are currently (2003) awaiting restoration. *Lens of Sutton collection*

Electric

The new Waterloo *c*1921, with electric trains at Platforms 1-4. By this time the electric services were running from here to Hounslow via the loop line, to Hampton Court and to Wimbledon via Putney. Plans to electrify the line to Guildford via Effingham Junction would not be realised until Southern days. *Lens of Sutton collection*

The LSWR's three-car electric units, designed by Arthur Jones, the company's Chief Electrical Engineer, were first introduced in 1915 for use on the line to Wimbledon via Putney. Unit E40, in sage-green livery, heads a second three-car unit past Cromer Road signalbox on a local service *c*1920. *R. C. Stumpf collection*

Above:
Three-car unit E7 on the north side of Surbiton station, forming a train for Waterloo *c*1922. With its iron decking, brick supports and arches, the bridge in the background remains a distinctive feature of this stretch of line. *R. C. Stumpf collection*

Below:
Unit E73 running with a second unit on the line to Hampton Court *c*1922. These units were quite dangerous for the motorman, as all circuits and relay equipment were live and open, staff having to watch what they touched, unless they wanted a 'shocking' experience! *R. C. Stumpf collection*

Unit E2 on the Hounslow loop line *c*1921, showing the motor end of the unit. This stock was somewhat dated in design, being panelled and featuring droplights and compartments not unlike those on Panter steam stock. *R. C. Stumpf collection*

Durnsford Road power station and car depot *c*1930, showing the inclined line to the power house, which ran between the high chimneys of the building. Built in 1914 and opened in 1915, the station provided the power for the company's first electrified lines. It would be closed and demolished in the late 1960s. *Lens of Sutton collection*

A District electric train of 'A' stock stops at Southfields station with a service for Wimbledon *c*1908. From the mid-19th century the LSWR and the District Railway had run joint services along the line from Putney to Wimbledon, and it was the District Railway's electrification in 1905 that prompted the LSWR to follow suit. *Lens of Sutton collection*

Waterloo & City car No 3 in the sidings at Waterloo, *c*1900, in its original livery with yellow straw lining, this stock was not replaced until 1940 when the new Bulleid stock came into service. *Ian Allan Library*

Left:
A rare scene at the line's Waterloo terminus *c*1930, showing a single Dick, Kerr car about to set off for Bank station. *R. C. Stumpf collection*

Below left:
The Drummond Bo-Bo electric locomotive built originally for shunting the Waterloo & City Railway. Built in 1898, it was transferred in 1915 to Durnsford Road, Wimbledon, for shunting the coal sidings at the power station, where it is seen at work in 1959 as SR No 74S. *John Scott-Morgan collection*

Below:
The second electric locomotive, built shortly after the Bo-Bo, was this four-wheeler, for working the power-station sidings at Waterloo on the Waterloo & City Railway. Seen at Waterloo underground-car depot on 4 June 1938 as SR No 75S, this locomotive is now preserved in Southern brown livery at the National Railway Museum and is one of the two oldest surviving electric locomotives in Britain. *John Scott-Morgan collection*

LSWR 10-ton van No 1408 in its distinctive livery of chocolate brown with white lettering, grey roof and white-rimmed tyres. Built in 1911, it would be withdrawn in November 1946. *John Scott-Morgan collection*

Goods wagons and services

Used on the Somerset & Dorset Joint Railway, road van No 750 shows both Midland and LSWR influence in its design. Most of this stock would be withdrawn by the late 1930s. *John Scott-Morgan collection*

Above:
Six-wheel sleeper wagon No 183, based at Redbridge Sleeper Works at Southampton, with a demonstration load of chaired sleepers in early Southern days *c*1924. It would remain in traffic until September 1930. *John Scott-Morgan collection*

Single bolster wagon No 9896 loaded with rails as part of an engineering train at Bridgwater (S&DJR) *c*1912. These wooden-underframed wagons were built in large numbers by most companies to take a load of 10 tons, most lasting in traffic until the 1930s. *R. Carpenter collection*

Five-plank open wagon No 13931, fitted with coil-spring axleboxes, pictured *c*1920. These tarpaulin-fitted high-bar wagons were built in large numbers from the 1890s, most lasting into the late 1930s and many becoming engineers' wagons.
R. Carpenter collection

A 15-ton LSWR eight-plank high-bar open — No 6641 — with long wheelbase, seen *c*1920. These opens of a modern design were used to transport crated and manufactured goods. *John Scott-Morgan collection*

Engineers' bogie bolster wagon No 455, built to transport rails on permanent-way trains, *c*1902. The wagon has American-style bogies with a wheel-screw brake mechanism. *R. Carpenter collection*

'E330' class saddle tank No 330 on shunting duties *c*1890, with an interesting array of wagons behind. The road van next to the locomotive is of an early pattern with 'birdcage' roof and large van-type side doors; the wagons behind this range from a three-plank stone open to two four-plank opens. *Ian Allan Library*

Right:
Adams 'O2' 0-4-4T No 200, running bunker-first with a freight from Holes Bay Junction, near Poole on 9 August 1901. A good photograph that illustrates the make-up of a local freight of this period. *Lens of Sutton collection*

Below:
Adams 'B4' 0-4-0T No 88 and breakdown train of runner, six-wheel steam crane and two riding vans, probably from the Beattie period, *c*1898. The locomotive is in lined holly green with the short-lived 'SWR' lettering style. *R. C. Stumpf collection*

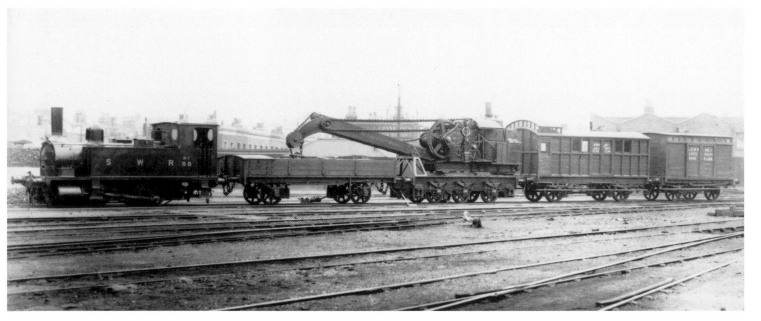

The exterior of Southampton Docks station *c*1910. This building, which still stands, is a good example of the work of William Tite. It and a similar structure at Nine Elms were the gateways to the London & Southampton Railway and represent the style and concept of a company at the dawn of railway history. *R. C. Stumpf collection*

Docks and shipping

The platforms of Southampton Docks station in the late 1890s, with passenger trains awaiting departure. A trio of Adams tanks stand at the head of their trains; on the left is a Radial 4-4-2T, in the centre a 'T1' 0-4-4T and on the right an 'O2' 0-4-4T, with a train of Great Western Dean stock. *Ian Allan Library*

100

The Royal Pier station at Southampton *c*1910, showing the buildings and pier with a train of short-underframed bogie stock at the platform. *R. C. Stumpf collection*

The Royal Pier again, this time *c*1908, showing paddle steamers moored at the quay and a train awaiting passengers at the station platform. It was from this pier that steamers ran to the Isle of Wight. *Lens of Sutton collection*

Lymington Pier *c*1910, with the paddle steamer *Solent* (built in 1902) awaiting passengers for the Isle of Wight. A train of non-corridor stock is just pulling into the station behind an Adams 4-4-0. *Lens of Sutton collection*

Lymington Pier again, *c*1911, with the same paddle steamer arriving from Cowes, Isle of Wight. A train headed by an Adams Radial 4-4-2T stands at the platform. *Lens of Sutton collection*

Portsmouth Harbour station *c*1914, seen from the landing stage, looking towards the naval dockyard, with a large quantity of luggage awaiting the steam packet to Ryde, Isle of Wight. In the middle distance is a line of LSWR bogie stock. *Ian Allan Library*

PS *Alliance*, built in 1855 by Ditchburn & Mare with atmospheric engines, which gave the vessel a top speed of 13 knots. She was used originally on the Southampton-Le Havre service and was later transferred to the Jersey-Granville-St Malo run. During her working life she was re-engined once and was finally sold for scrap in 1900, after 45 years' service. *Ian Allan Library*

PS *Southampton* had a long and varied working life. Built by Palmer of Jarrow in 1860, she was very advanced for her time and originally had two funnels but, after lengthening and rebuilding with a new boiler in 1880, emerged with just one. Employed thereafter on the Le Havre service, she was used for spectators at the Diamond Jubilee Naval Review in 1897, by which time she was a regular ship on the Channel Islands run. Sold to Messrs Yarrow for use as a floating hostel for their employees, she was finally broken up in the Netherlands in 1898. She is seen here entering Le Havre *c*1890. *Ian Allan Library*

Left:
The SS *Cherbourg* and her sister *Honfleur* were built in 1873 and worked for the LSWR and the Southern Railway for 57 years on cargo services out of Southampton. The *Cherbourg*, seen here *c*1890, would be sold by the Southern in 1930. *Ian Allan Library*

Below:
Built in 1910 by Cammell Laird at Birkenhead, TSS *Sarnia* was a turbine steamer of 1,500 gross tons and could reach 20 knots. She had a triple-screw arrangement with Parsons turbines. Given the Latin name for Guernsey, she spent most of her life on the Channel Islands service, but during World War 1 she was used by the military as a boarding vessel and came to grief on 12 September 1918, when she was torpedoed in the Mediterranean. *Ian Allan Library*

TSS *Alberta* was built by John Brown of Clydebank in 1900. The last of the LSWR's reciprocating-engined ships, the *Alberta* was used on Channel Island services until withdrawn in December 1929 by the Southern Railway, which sold her the following year to Greek owners. *Ian Allan Library*

The TSS *Princess Ena* was the only LSWR vessel with a royal name. Launched by Gourlay Bros on 25 May 1906, at which time she was the largest steamer owned by the LSWR, with a gross tonnage of 1,198, she had reciprocating engines (as opposed to turbines) and could reach 19 knots. On 3 August 1935 a fire broke out on board while she was on her regular passage from Jersey to St Malo, as a result of which she sank. *Ian Allan Library*

Dock tanks

No 108 *Cowes*, one of the 0-4-0ST locomotives built by Shanks in 1877 for use in Southampton Docks. Put on the duplicate list as No 0108 in 1904, the locomotive was withdrawn and sold in 1915. *Ian Allan Library*

Vulcan, an 0-4-0ST built in 1878 by Vulcan Foundry for the Southampton Dock Co. Numbered 118 upon acquisition by the LSWR in 1893, it would be sold by the Southern Railway in 1924. *Ian Allan Library*

Southampton Dock Co Hawthorn Leslie 0-4-0ST *Clausentum* at Southampton Dock shed *c*1900. It became No 457 with the LSWR in 1901 and was renumbered 0457 in 1908. Its sister, *Ironside*, survived into British Railways days on various light duties. *Ian Allan Library*

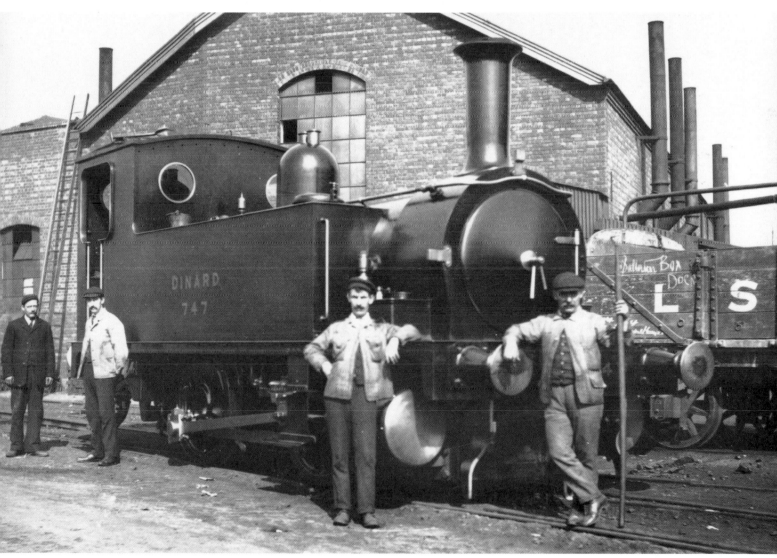

Class K14 0-4-0T No 747 *Dinard* at Southampton Docks *c*1910. Built at Nine Elms in 1908, these 0-4-0Ts were for many years the mainstay of the docks' locomotive fleet and survived well into British Railways days, a few examples of this type being still at work as late as the early 1960s. *Ian Allan Library*

A Beattie 'Vesuvius' class 2-4-0 tender locomotive at the old Nine Elms Works *c*1870s in its original livery of dark maroon with yellow-and-black lining. These locomotives originally burned coke rather than coal. The flywheel on the side of the long splasher was attached to a pump which worked a circulation system to keep the boiler filled with water when the locomotive was standing still. This system was later replaced by injectors. *R. C. Stumpf collection*

Locomotive workshops and sheds

Beattie 2-4-0 tender locomotive *Lacy* on the Dunn's traverser at Nine Elms Works *c*1870. The water-circulation boiler pump can be clearly seen behind the main splasher. *Ian Allan Library*

Drummond 4-2-2-0 No 369 in the repair shop at Nine Elms *c*1908. These four-cylinder locomotives were not very successful, being relegated to lesser duties by 1922 and withdrawn by the Southern Railway shortly after the Grouping. *Ian Allan Library*

By the early 20th century it had become clear that Nine Elms Works lacked the capacity to repair increasing volumes of locomotives and rolling stock and to build replacements. Towards the end of Drummond's time and in the early years of Urie's tenure a new works was planned, and this was built at Eastleigh in Hampshire, opening in two phases — the Carriage & Wagon Works in 1890/1 and the Locomotive Works in 1910, of which this is a general view, shortly after opening. The large building on the right is the administration block, still in use today. *Lens of Sutton collection*

Five o'clock at Eastleigh Works *c*1919 — a panoramic view of the main workshops and the fan of sidings serving them. *John Scott-Morgan collection*

Above:
A further view of the main workshops at Eastleigh *c*1919. This picture shows rows of tenders and wagons awaiting attention. In the foreground (left) is Drummond 'F13' 4-6-0 No 334, used at this time for goods traffic from Nine Elms to Southampton Docks; on the right an 'E330' class 0-6-0ST (probably a works shunter) stands dead at the head of a line of wagons. *Ian Allan Library*

Centre left:
'H15' No 335, nominally a Urie rebuild of a Drummond 'E14' 4-6-0, stands in the paintshop at Eastleigh Works on 24 April 1920 after an overhaul and repaint. This locomotive was 'rebuilt' in December 1914 and withdrawn in June 1959. *Ian Allan Library*

Lower left:
Drummond 'T9' 4-4-0 No 702 in original condition outside the works at Eastleigh *c*1912 after a heavy overhaul. This photograph shows the cab in detail and also the Drummond cross-tube firebox, which was later removed by Urie. *Ian Allan Library*

Above right:
On the dump at Eastleigh on 19 May 1923, a line of rebuilt Beattie outside-frame 0-6-0 goods locomotives — Nos 0229, 0380 and 288A — await cutting-up after a full working life. *Ian Allan Library*

Class F13 4-6-0 No 334, built at Nine Elms in 1905, passes Eastleigh Works *c*1920 with a heavy freight bound for Southampton. These lacklustre 4-6-0s were withdrawn soon after the Grouping in 1923. *Ian Allan Library*

Beattie 0-6-0 goods No 278A and ex-Southampton Dock Co 0-4-0ST No 118 *Vulcan* in front of the coal stage at Eastleigh shed *c*1920. The LSWR had very distinctive coaling stages which had an under-cover coal-sorting area with chutes to decant the coal into locomotive tenders and bunkers. *Ian Allan Library*

Above right:
Adams '135' class 4-4-0 No 146, built by Beyer Peacock in 1880, provides the backdrop for a group of fitters and the shedmaster posing for a photograph *c*1890. The locomotive is about to be lifted to facilitate running repairs. *Ian Allan Library*

Right:
An early Adams Radial, No 377, undergoes some basic repairs at Guildford shed *c*1920, by which time these locomotives were nearing the end of their long and varied careers. This example has a Drummond chimney and smokebox door. *R. C. Stumpf collection*

Class A12 'Jubilee' 0-4-2 tender locomotive No 632 being coaled at Eastleigh *c*1919, showing the ramp ready for use. Built by Neilson in 1893 and withdrawn in August 1937, the locomotive is seen here in Drummond condition. *Ian Allan Library*

Civil engineering — bridges and viaducts

Left:
Class C8 4-4-0 No 177 crosses Meldon Viaduct with an up train on 14 July 1924. This impressive structure, which still exists today, was the highest point on both the LSWR and later the Southern Railway. There are, in fact, two viaducts built side by side, as the line west of Okehampton was originally single, a second line being built later, when the North Devon and Cornwall lines were extended. *Ian Allan Library*

Below:
Fartherford Viaduct *c*1914, with a Drummond 4-4-0 (probably a 'K10') crossing with an express from Exeter. This structure is built of local stone and makes an imposing sight in the hills around Okehampton. *Ian Allan Library*

Above right:
The three-span girder bridge over Little Petherick Creek, near Padstow, photographed *c*1920. This bridge still stands and is used today by cyclists riding the Camel Trail to Bodmin.
Ian Allan Library

Below right:
The swing bridge over the River Plym on the Turnchapel branch in Plymouth. 'O2' 0-4-4T No 218 crosses with a mixed passenger train of Panter non-corridor bogie stock and a 'Gate' set at the rear on its way to Turnchapel on 28 June 1924. *Ian Allan Library*

Signalling

The timber-built signalbox at Corfe Castle on the Swanage branch, seen in Southern days but still in LSWR condition. The 'box is a mixture of early LSWR practice, with small windows and timber framing, and later practice, with the large window with small panes looking out along the line from the door. *R. C. Stumpf collection*

Tisted 'box on the Meon Valley line. An example of late-LSWR design — constructed (mostly of brick) with large timber-framed windows and a semi-sheltered entrance porch — again seen in early SR days. *Ian Allan Library*

Above right:
Wimbledon South 'box, with its brick base and timber upper-glazed lever room. This design represents the middle period of LSWR signalbox design, between the timber-framed 'boxes of the early days and the later substantial brick structures. A Beattie outside-framed 0-6-0 goods locomotive — No 273A of the '273' class, built by Beyer Peacock in 1872 — shunts the coal yard on 11 March 1922. *Ian Allan Library*

Right:
Wimbledon Signal Works, with No 289A — a '273' class outside-framed 0-6-0 built by Beyer Peacock in 1872 — shunting the works yard on 10 June 1920. Wimbledon Signal & Civil Engineer's Works produced anything from signalling equipment to tanks for water towers, for use all over the LSWR system. The works still exists and is still used as an engineers' store. *Ian Allan Library*

Above left:
Feltham 'box and level crossing *c*1900. This is an example of an early timber structure with brick base, dating from the middle years of the 19th century. *Lens of Sutton collection*

Left:
An impressive gantry of pressure pneumatic signals near Winchfield *c*1966, shortly before their replacement with electric-light signals as part of the Bournemouth-line electrification. Linked to track circuiting and based on American practice, these gantries were in evidence at intervals along the quadrupled section of line from London to Basingstoke. *R. C. Stumpf collection*

Above left:
Up starter and shunt signals 'off' (cleared) at Alresford on the Mid-Hants line on 6 August 1955. *John Scott-Morgan collection*

Above right:
Siding starting signals at Fareham on 12 October 1957. Note that this interesting lattice-post signal has lower-quadrant arms with white circles edged with black rings. *John Scott-Morgan collection*

Stations and staff

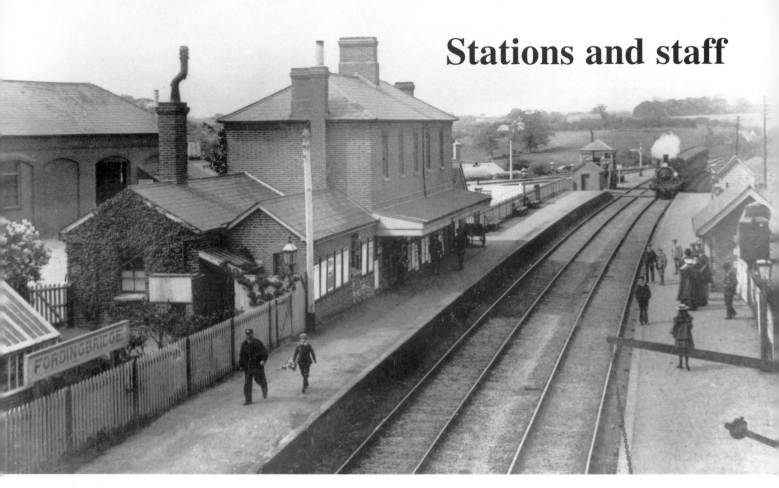

Fordingbridge, on the line from Salisbury to Poole, *c*1890s, with a local service about to enter the station. This is an example of the late-Georgian-style architecture to be found on the early LSWR in the shape of rather plain-looking brick or stone station buildings. *R. Carpenter collection*

Verwood, on the line from Salisbury to Poole, looking towards Salisbury, *c*1900, with the station staff posing on the platform. This is a mid-Victorian structure with brick station building and timber signalbox and station shelters. *R. Carpenter collection*

Left:
Liss, on the Portsmouth Direct line, looking towards Guildford, *c*1900. This station, built by Thomas Brassey as a speculative venture, was slightly different from normal LSWR practice of the 1850s, with a brick-built main building and timber awnings and platform shelters. *Lens of Sutton collection*

Basingstoke, at the junction of the London–Bournemouth and West of England main lines, *c*1914. This picture shows the third station (which still exists today), with its substantial brick building, long awnings and lengthy platforms. The buildings on the far left are all that remains of the second station built in the 1850s, behind which stands the Great Western station on the line to Reading. *R. C. Stumpf collection*

Above left:
An early view of Lapford station, on the North Devon line from Exeter to Barnstaple, *c*1880s, showing the station building, built of brick with cement facing, and the staff. *Lens of Sutton collection*

Above:
Members of the station staff at Romsey *c*1900. This station was the junction for the original line from Bishopstoke (Eastleigh) to Salisbury. This photograph shows the full complement of staff needed at this time to run a large country station, from the stationmaster to the boys who worked in the goods office. *R. C. Stumpf collection*

Left:
Bere Ferrers, on the main line from Okehampton to Plymouth, *c*1910, showing the stone-and-brick station with its late-period awning and steel-girder footbridge. *Lens of Sutton collection*

The staff at St Denys *c*1911, posed in their best uniforms for the photographer. On the main line from London to Southampton, St Denys was then an important local station and junction with the line along the coast to Portsmouth. *Lens of Sutton collection*

Probably the worst accident ever to befall the LSWR was the Salisbury disaster, which occurred on 1 July 1906. Attempting to negotiate Salisbury station's curved track at high speed, the Plymouth–Waterloo boat train became derailed and smashed into two other trains waiting on adjacent roads, one being a local headed by a Beattie goods, the other a milk train. Among the 28 fatalities were the driver and fireman of 'L12' No 421, heading the boat train, the fireman of the Beattie goods and the guard of the milk train.
Lens of Sutton collection

Mishaps

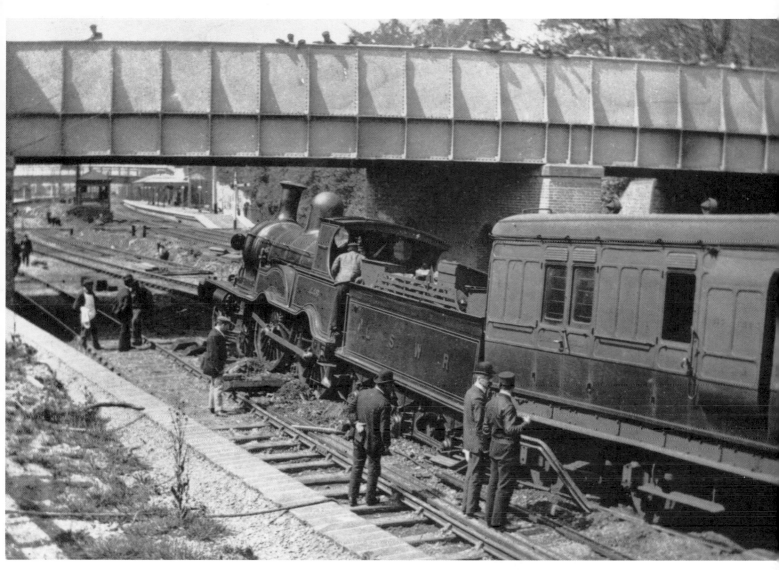

Derailment at Farnborough Main in the 1900s, with Adams '460' 4-4-0 No 448 (in Drummond livery) and a train of Panter stock off the road at a set of catch points.
Lens of Sutton collection

'T1' 0-4-4T No 65 after running off the end of a siding at Camberley in the 1900s.
The locomotive has come to rest on the road at the bottom of the railway embankment.
Lens of Sutton collection

Road transport

Left:
Unloading a train of bogie carriage stock at Botley *c*1910 — an interesting photograph, with LSWR and private road wagons much in evidence. *Lens of Sutton collection*

Below left:
Hustle and bustle at Swanwick goods yard *c*1900, with road delivery wagons much in evidence unloading a van train, and the yard full of general-merchandise wagons awaiting attention. *Lens of Sutton collection*

Right:
A Thornycroft petrol bus in use on the Hythe service *c*1908. These vehicles were employed on a number of routes, including the Farnham–Haslemere service.
Lens of Sutton collection

A Clarkson steam bus at Nine Elms Works *c*1905. This was one of four such vehicles purchased for the Exeter–Chagford and New Milton–Lymington bus services and was tried on various routes before being sold in 1908. *Lens of Sutton collection*

Rebuilt 'T14' 4-6-0 No 445 runs through Clapham Junction *c*1925 with a train of ex-LSWR carriage stock. The LSWR ceased to exist at midnight on 31 December 1922, whereafter the new Southern Railway came into being and a new era in railway history began. *R. C. Stumpf collection*

The formation of the Southern Railway

Horsley station on 4 April 1925 — two years after the LSWR's demise — but the stock is still in pre-Grouping liveries, even if the 'M7' is in Southern green. *R. C. Stumpf collection*